S.M.A.R.T. AI FOR BUSINESS

SAVE TIME AND INCREASE PROFITS WITH PERSONALIZED MARKETING STRATEGIES, EFFECTIVE RECRUITING TACTICS, AND EASY TO IMPLEMENT CHATBOT TECHNOLOGY

© **Copyright 2024 - All rights reserved.**

The content contained within this book may not be reproduced, duplicated or transmitted without direct written permission from the author or the publisher.

Under no circumstances will any blame or legal responsibility be held against the publisher, or author, for any damages, reparation, or monetary loss due to the information contained within this book, either directly or indirectly.

Legal Notice:

This book is copyright protected. It is only for personal use. You cannot amend, distribute, sell, use, quote or paraphrase any part, or the content within this book, without the consent of the author or publisher.

Disclaimer Notice:

Please note the information contained within this document is for educational and entertainment purposes only. All effort has been executed to present accurate, up to date, reliable, complete information. No warranties of any kind are declared or implied. Readers acknowledge that the author is not engaged in the rendering of legal, financial, medical or professional advice. The content within this book has been derived from various sources. Please consult a licensed professional before attempting any techniques outlined in this book.

By reading this document, the reader agrees that under no circumstances is the author responsible for any losses, direct or indirect, that are incurred as a result of the use of the information contained within this document, including, but not limited to, errors, omissions, or inaccuracies.

TABLE OF CONTENTS

Introduction	7
CHAPTER 1: STARTING WITH A STRONG FOUNDATION	11
Assessing Your AI Readiness	
The Need for a Self-Assessment	14
Checklists Tailored to Your AI Strategy	16
Aligning AI Goals With Business Objectives	19
AI Accelerator	22

PART I
AI POWERED CHATBOTS FOR BUSINESS

CHAPTER 2: CRAFTING A SUCCESSFUL CHATBOT STRATEGY	27
Unwritten Laws	28
The Power of Conversational AI	29
Building Your Chatbot	32
Selecting the Right Tools: Quality Over Quantity	35
AI Accelerator	40
CHAPTER 3: PRIVACY, SECURITY, AND ETHICS FOR CHATBOTS	43
Data Privacy in Conversations	44
Navigating Ethical Challenges in Chatbot Design	49
AI Accelerator: SWOT Analysis	52
CHAPTER 4: THE CHATBOT CHRONICLES	57
Success in the Land of Algorithms	
The Need for Chatbots	58
Chatbot Implementation Process	60
Chatbot Functionality	62

Addressing Integration Obstacles ... 62
Measurable Results ... 64
Post-Implementation Challenges ... 65
AI Accelerator ... 68

PART II

PERSONALIZATION IN MARKETING WITH AI

CHAPTER 5: CRAFTING A HYPERPERSONALIZED MARKETING STRATEGY ... 75
The Role of AI in Modern Marketing ... 76
Hyperpersonalized Marketing in Everyday Life ... 78
Implementing AI for Personalized Customer Journeys ... 82
Tool Selection: Balancing Cost and Capability ... 84
AI Accelerator ... 86

CHAPTER 6: ETHICS AND SECURITY IN AI-DRIVEN MARKETING ... 91
Protecting Customer Data in Marketing Campaigns ... 93
Threat Mitigation Strategies ... 96
The Need for Regular Security Audits and Updates ... 99
Ethical Considerations in Personalization ... 104
Ethical Implications of Data Sourcing ... 109
AI Accelerator ... 112

CHAPTER 7: THE ART OF PERSONALIZATION ... 119
Marketing Success Stories
Your Needs Assessment ... 121
Coca-Cola ... 122
Starbucks ... 123
Nike ... 125
Agency Pure ... 126
AI Accelerator ... 128

PART III
AI POWERED RECRUITMENT SOLUTIONS

CHAPTER 8: TRANSFORMING HIRING WITH AI	135
The Modern Recruitment Landscape and the Remote Revolution	137
Steps to Integrate AI Into Your Recruitment Process	138
Choosing the Perfect AI Recruitment Solution	143
AI Accelerator	146
CHAPTER 9: TRUST IN RECRUITMENT	151
AI Ethics and Data Security	
Ensuring Candidate Data Privacy	152
Best Practices	156
Transparent Data Handling Processes	158
Training Data: The Origins of AI Bias	160
AI Accelerator	164

PART IV
BUILDING AND SUSTAINING YOUR AI STRATEGY

CHAPTER 10: MONITORING, MEASUREMENT, AND ROI	169
Key Metrics to Gauge AI Success	171
Evaluating ROI: Beyond Just Numbers	174
Continuously Refining Your AI Strategy	177
Lessons From Spotify's Recommendation AI	179
AI Accelerator	180
CHAPTER 11: ADOPTING FUTURE AI DEVELOPMENTS	185
Ensuring Your AI Solutions Stay Relevant	187
Building a Culture of AI-Driven Innovation and Adaptability	191
AI Accelerator	195

Conclusion 201
References 207

INTRODUCTION

This is the age of artificial intelligence (AI). Buckle up.

We're at a point in our existence where the everyday use of AI is no longer a matter of if or when. It is rapidly becoming a transformative force that is being compared to another industrial revolution. For the past 200 years, the business world has been on a steady evolutionary trajectory, driven by integrating new technologies. But, it is fair to say that nothing that has come before has reached the rapidity and sheer scope of change that the integration of AI into business strategies is creating. The opportunities for efficiency and growth are significant and even essential for business survival in the foreseeable future.

In 2022, Forbes estimated the AI market to be worth around $86 billion (Haan, 2023). Following recent developments in the AI sector, the market is expected to be worth more than $400 billion by the year 2027. According to the same survey, this is partly attributed to the fact that at least 60% of businesses have invested in, or are working on implementing AI in their operations to improve productivity (Haan, 2023).

While AI can rejuvenate your business and help you become more efficient and competitive, implementing it can come with a hefty price tag. Many AI models can be contingent on an army of tech wizards with job skills akin to sorcery. Likewise, there are models available to you that will require substantial infrastructure and Silicon Valley budget allocations. These are almost exclusively the preserve of bigger, well-established enterprises and corporations.

And this may be where it all started, but the constant, quick-paced evolution of the technology has diversified and expanded to allow everyone a seat at the AI table. Rest assured, you can lay hold of competitive edges and get customized strategies and solutions for the challenges your business is facing. The right fit is out there for you, and this book is designed to help you get it by giving you step-by-step methods, practical tools, and tangible resources to help make your business's AI journey lucrative and safe.

Should your small or medium-sized business transition to AI? Take a look at the data. According to Charest (2023), at least 60% of small businesses that have integrated AI or some form of automation are working more efficiently, and more importantly, have saved a lot of time in their business processes. The published report, "Small Business Now: An AI Awakening," sought the opinion of some 500 small and medium-sized business owners across the US on the role of AI in their businesses, and how the transition had affected their operations. Interestingly enough, there was overwhelming support for AI, with at least 91% of the correspondents admitting that their businesses enjoyed more success since the AI integration.

Think about your current market. AI-driven analytics provides businesses with valuable insight into consumer behavior, market trends, and operational efficiency. With such insight, you can make better decisions that impact your profitability. It could be anything from managing your supply chain to optimizing strategies or setting the right prices. With access to the right data, AI can also help you explore new growth opportunities to diversify.

But we all know our business is only as good as our people. Finding and hiring the right personnel is a demanding and continuous process for any company. According to Forbes Business Council, the average hire requires a recruiter 23 hours of screening and setting up interviews (Staffing Referrals, 2020). But what if it didn't? AI is transforming the recruiting and hiring process. The pool of available desirable applicants is not infinite—it's a competitive field for your human resources (HR) department or person. This is an AI train you cannot afford to miss.

And chatbots! The leaps in return on investment (ROI) in companies that implement the right chatbot are staggering! This makes sense, because chatbots generally assure users of faster response times, on average three times faster than customer support agents (Cherniak, 2023). Suffice to say, these are the droids you're looking for. You will need some fundamental understanding of conversational AI to craft or procure a chatbot tailored to your needs and aligned with your objectives. Read on and let the games begin.

Finally, every AI function comes with its own ethical concerns and security issues. You must gain a fundamental knowledge of what these are, not only to continue to be an ethical and secure company but also to protect your company from the consequences of violations. You will find information and resources for a firm foundation within these pages.

Overall, the informational roadmap for integrating AI into your business life is presented in a way that will dovetail into a framework that most businesses are familiar with: S.M.A.R.T. It's about managing your objectives in a way that defines **specific goals** that are **measurable, attainable, realistic** for where your business is right now, and **time-bound** so that you are not still trying to get the processes off the ground before the last syllable of recorded time (Leonard & Watts, 2022).

In the coming chapters, you will find the information you need to navigate through AI's dynamic terrain. These practical steps will help you arrive at your sweet spot—the place where you can measure your ROI. No matter your current size or budget constraints, there is something in the world of AI that will help your business right now. At the end of the day, it's not just about choosing the best AI but also finding a perfect fit for both your business and your bottom line. That fit is out there, and it is attainable.

CHAPTER 1: STARTING WITH A STRONG FOUNDATION
ASSESSING YOUR AI READINESS

> *AI is a tool. The choice about how it gets deployed is ours.*
>
> — OREN ETZIONI

Everyone's excited about AI. There are lots of opportunities for integration, opportunities that will take your business to the next level. If you're thinking in terms of improved efficiency or value addition, you have to explore AI at some point, and this leads us to the most important question: Are you ready for AI?

Despite the widely documented benefits of using AI, it can only be as good as the foundation on which you set it up. Think of AI like a computer program. If you feed it the wrong data, you cannot expect it to give you accurate results. And even though AI can learn and get better on its own (a concept that continues to amaze), you still have to get the fundamentals right, and the most important of them all is assessing your preparedness.

To help ensure you're starting your journey into AI on the right footing, let's take a look at the benefits of being prepared and how to avoid common pitfalls. There are some best practices already established that will help your team. The wheel has already been invented; you just need to make adjustments to tailor available tools to your goals and start to roll with them.

Consider the following cases:

- A small ecommerce business implements AI for personalized recommendations without assessing the quality of its existing customer data. Conducting a data quality assessment before implementation would have indicated the need to cleanse and preprocess its data to ensure it was accurate and relevant to its current needs before a new AI's implementation took off.
- A midsize manufacturing company adopts AI-driven automation without adequately training employees on how to work with the new technology. An honest self-assessment of its workforce and management would have prioritized training programs to ensure they were well-versed in using and maintaining its AI system, making for a much smoother integration and far less stress on its most valuable resource—its people.
- A financial services startup implements AI for customer account management without assessing

potential security risks. A comprehensive security assessment before deployment would have indicated the need for robust encryption, access controls, and regular security audits. You don't want to know you needed these yesterday.
- A marketing agency implements AI for campaign optimization without setting realistic performance expectations. A preemptive self-assessment would have indicated the need to clearly define goals and communicate them transparently to stakeholders, and to regularly evaluate and adjust expectations based on outcomes.
- A small software development company implements AI features in its product line without considering scalability issues for future growth. A scalability assessment would have helped to ensure the AI solution could handle the increased volume and user load so that when growth starts accelerating, everyone and everything is onboard and ready to ride the express success train.

The truth is, AI can make your business much more efficient. However, if your business setup isn't built for efficiency, you'll be efficiently churning out inefficiency. In the business world, there's nothing as bad as being so good at failure.

The lesson here is that you must get all your ducks in a row and make certain you organize your thoughts and actions before implementing AI so that all the pieces will fall into place at the right time.

The Need for a Self-Assessment

You can assess your preparedness for AI by answering the following questions:

- Does your business have the quality of data your AI model needs? Is that data readily accessible to you? Let's say you outsource some of your data management tasks to third parties, what must you do to obtain that data and avail it for your AI?
- Do you have the necessary computing resources and other infrastructure required to effectively implement AI in your business? This evaluation means checking if you have the right hardware, for example, high-performance processors and memory capacities. Similarly, check if you have the software frameworks in place and whether your networking capabilities are conducive to AI operations.

  Think about data storage solutions. Do you have the resources necessary to accommodate the vast datasets that will be required for training your AI model? Do you have scalable cloud services or on-premises infrastructure to support the computational demands of your AI? This evaluation will go a long way in your preparedness survey, making sure that your existing resources are not overwhelmed and can comfortably measure up against the requirements of your AI model. Remember, the goal here is to match seamless implementation with optimal performance to get the most value from your AI.

- Where do you stand on data literacy? Given access to your raw data, can you draw any meaningful conclusions or deductions from it? Data literacy will be crucial in addressing and navigating the complexities that arise once you implement AI into your business model. Ideally, data literacy sets the foundation on which you or your team can extract insights and make informed decisions from the data in your possession.

  For example, given access to raw data, do you understand how the AI will analyze patterns, identify correlations, and extract meaningful conclusions, especially within the limitations of the data provided? More importantly, what are the ethical considerations surrounding data usage and privacy that must be taken into account?

- How do you handle the ethical or legal concerns that will arise when you implement AI? For example, how do you deal with the fact that implementing AI might mean some tasks or job roles become redundant? What happens when your AI model discriminates or happens to favor some of your customers?
- What if your employees do not wish to embrace AI, or even if they do, you still face some resistance?

You can preempt many of these concerns by taking steps to ease the integration process. If you're well-prepared, you can expect better outcomes with AI, for example, smoother implementation and integration in your business model, personnel that see the benefit and are excited about the new resources, and ultimately, improvements in cost efficiency and ROI.

This is how you set your business apart from other small to medium businesses. Taking the time for a strong self-assessment will set you up to identify and plan for the changes needed to successfully compete in a rapidly evolving environment. It is hands down the best way to optimize your investment in AI.

Checklists Tailored to Your AI Strategy

By now, it's clear you need an effective AI-preparedness strategy to help you streamline the implementation process. Here are some important questions that can guide you through this process. Because every business is unique, you should always tailor your checklist according to your business needs.

- Is there sufficient or relevant demand from your customers to warrant the implementation you're about to initiate?
- What are the immediate impacts or changes that this integration will have on your business and your customers?

- How much time and effort must be committed to this process?
- Do you need to make custom changes to your business model, and how do they affect your brand?
- How does this implementation affect or influence your typical customer journey?

This assessment will help you discern how to proceed with the implementation. Of course, the answers won't always be favorable, but that's alright. Where the answers are not affirmative, you realize the opportunities that must be addressed. In addition to ideas and strategies, you must resolve issues that need to be discussed with your team or other relevant parties. The point here is to understand not just your preparedness for AI but also how the inner sanctum of your business operates, efficiently or otherwise.

From your assessment above, you can now sit down and create a strategic plan for implementing AI. This follows the same process as creating a business plan. You must understand your strengths and weaknesses, assess your market, and study what your competitors are doing, among other things. Here are some simple steps that can guide you:

- First and foremost, build an effective team to help you take this project forward. Your team should understand the need for AI and see the bigger picture as you do. Agree to embrace your new collective identity as pioneers and visionaries, and have some fun with it. The road forward is rarely straight and barrier-free, which makes getting there all the more sweet when you finally turn on the AI lights.

- Set clear objectives for AI integration. What's the purpose? How does that purpose align with your core business objectives, vision, and mission? This may seem too fundamental to mention, but you may find times when you need to pull back to this basic plumb line to avoid distractions.
- Assess the availability of data, and more importantly, the quality of data you'll be feeding into the AI model. In this case, you're trying to make sure your AI model is effective in the role it will perform in your business. For availability, consider the volume and accessibility of data relevant to the model's objectives. Do you have sufficient data for training, validation, and testing? On quality, you have to make sure the data is accurate, relevant, and aptly represents your interests. This is how you weed out biases, errors, and inconsistencies that could skew your outcomes.
- What resources will you need to make this process a success? What do you have to buy, and which items can you outsource?
- Are you setting up your AI model on the cloud, or are you running the entire operation on-premises? Running your model on the cloud helps you utilize vast computational resources provided by cloud services. You'll enjoy scalability, flexibility, and accessibility, which make it easier to efficiently

process large-scale tasks and accommodate the demands of your business as they evolve. This is the approach that most businesses use, since running your operation on-premise could attract more costs, and require resources that become quite expensive in the long run.
- If you are in discussions with the vendors, ask for a proof of concept suitable for *your* business model. Don't implement an AI solution based on the use cases presented to you. Proof of concept demonstrates the AI model in operation, which can help you decide whether it's suitable for your business or not.
- What steps must you take to meet the relevant compliance and regulatory demands, if any? For example, what's the legal position of implementing AI in your state? Federal law might not have widely encompassing legislation on AI, but some states do.

Even as you think of the possible ROI, the biggest step in your plan is how to handle or manage the impending changes. This is where many businesses struggle. Change is inevitable. To build resilience in your business, you must prepare for changes.

Aligning AI Goals With Business Objectives

Here's one point that many small business owners tend to overlook—your AI model is not here to work, it's here to work for you. AI becomes ineffective if it does not align with your business objectives, mission, and vision. Since AI wasn't present in the formative days of your business, how can it know your needs, vision, and mission? It must get this information from you.

Are you trying to improve customer satisfaction, improve product quality, or enhance your operational efficiency? These are common goals many businesses work toward, but not necessarily what will apply to yours. You do get the picture, though? Knowledge of your business needs sets the tone for your implementation strategy. With clear business goals, you can then discuss how the AI model can solve each of your concerns. For example, are you going to automate some tasks, or use AI for forecasting?

What are your key performance indicators (KPIs)?

The point here is to establish specific metrics to measure specific goals, for example, customer retention, revenue growth projections, cost savings, or anything else you're trying to improve with AI. Clear KPIs make it easier to track the effectiveness of your AI initiatives, and more importantly, map the way forward for sustainable improvement. Note that it's easier for AI vendors, or your technical staff, to build custom solutions for you if they know what you're working toward. With this in mind, make your intentions and desired outcomes clear to them.

Finally, follow agile methodology when implementing AI. Agile is a project management strategy where you break down projects and processes into smaller, manageable phases or milestones. Agile sets the tone for effective collaboration and phased improvement, which, ultimately, supports your need for sustainable growth. The concept is quite simple: You plan for each phase, execute the necessary steps, and evaluate outcomes (Włodarczyk, 2023).

Your business operates in a constantly evolving environment, and you attend to customers whose needs are just as dynamic. In response, you must continually evaluate your business model to ensure that your business initiatives align with the evolving business environment and customer needs. This is how you stay ahead of the competition.

Once you implement AI, don't just let it run on autopilot. Create time to analyze key metrics, monitor performance, and discuss pertinent issues arising with your team to ensure the AI integration doesn't stray far away from your business goals, mission, and vision. Agile methodology helps you run a business that's not just flexible, but also responsive to the changes happening around you. This is also how you get the utmost value from your AI.

You might not be able to preempt everything in business, but you can put plans in place to capitalize on the opportunities that AI brings your way. And the opportunities continue to mount. Small businesses are increasingly using AI-powered chatbots. "Chatbots may save as much as 2.5 billion hours per year in customer interaction by streamlining processes and freeing up human resources for more difficult duties" (Tiffany, 2023). AI implementation in small businesses can lead to significant cost savings. An Accenture (2017) report estimated that AI could contribute up to $1.2 trillion in annual business value by 2035. Now, that's a market you'd definitely want to be a player in, right?

AI Accelerator

Here's a simple template you can use to assess your AI preparedness by assessing your current tech setup, knowledge of AI, and how they align with your business goals. Your readiness level increases as you check off more items. You can tweak this template to concerns specific to your business model and mark them as follows:

- **Not Started:** No progress or activity in the category.
- **Beginner:** Some initial steps taken, but more work needed.
- **Intermediate:** Moderate progress with room for improvement.
- **Advanced:** Significant achievements and a high level of readiness.

Mark an "X" in the appropriate column, based on your current status in each category. The goal is to have more checks in the advanced column to indicate a higher level of readiness.

Current Tech Setup				
Readiness Categories	**Not Started**	**Beginner**	**Intermediate**	**Advanced**
Website or online presence				
Ecommerce capabilities				
Cloud services usage				
Point-of-sale systems				

Knowledge of AI				
Readiness Categories	**Not Started**	**Beginner**	**Intermediate**	**Advanced**
Awareness of AI				
Basic AI applications				
Knowledge of data security				

	Business Goals			
Readiness Categories	Not Started	Beginner	Intermediate	Advanced
Increased efficiency				
Improved customer experience				
Data-driven decision-making				
Gain competitive advantage				

Now that you're equipped with the foundational knowledge to assess your AI readiness, it's time to delve deep into the world of chatbots—tools that can revolutionize your customer experience. In the next chapter, we'll guide you through designing an impeccable AI chatbot strategy tailor-made for your business.

PART ONE

AI POWERED CHATBOTS FOR BUSINESS

CHAPTER 2: CRAFTING A SUCCESSFUL CHATBOT STRATEGY

> *The advance of technology is based on making it fit so that you don't really even notice it, so it's part of everyday life.*
>
> — BILL GATES

Did you know that 74% of users prefer chatbots when they need answers to simple questions? (FHG, 2022).

Have you ever made a customer service call that went smoothly? It was efficient, saved you time, and you got exactly what you needed without being put on hold–or going through a daunting list of menus or having to start your request over and over because you are in the twilight zone of endless transfers. If this sounds familiar, you encountered a well-programmed chatbot interaction!

When a customer calls your business for the first time, they are starting the initial interaction that will have profound implications for the relationship that develops thereafter, or even if there will be one. They have made first contact. This is a concept that is well-defined in other domains. Anthropologists have written extensively on first interactions between different cultures; and who among us has not seen or read classic science fiction stories of first meetings between humans and extraterrestrials?

All these scenarios real and fiction share some common variables that apply to the business world. Let's call them unwritten laws of first contact. Across all domains, communicating effectively and understanding the other party is crucial. Misunderstandings can lead to conflict and dissatisfaction (and occasionally a hostile takeover of the planet, depending on who you are trying to communicate with).

Unwritten Laws

When we talk about a chatbot strategy, you have to think beyond technology; it's about creating a human-like and personalized experience. A conversational flow that feels natural and caters to user needs will always enhance engagement. Utilizing machine learning algorithms, chatbots can learn from user interactions and continuously improve their performance over time. Your challenge, therefore, is striking the right balance between automation and human intervention. This is crucial, as it ensures that complex issues are seamlessly escalated to your team when necessary. In this way, you don't just address pressing issues at a personal level, but also preserve the human touch in customer interactions. So, the most important question is: How do you get there?

A successful chatbot strategy will be crucial in harnessing the transformative potential of conversational AI and ensuring the positive impact that delivers a win-win situation for both customers and business owners. The first step involves understanding your specific needs, to make sure that your chatbots don't just address them but also align with your overall goals and vision for the business. This analysis will help you identify key areas where the chatbot can add value, such as customer support, lead generation, or internal processes. From there, you can set the foundation for a targeted and effective strategy.

Once your objectives are defined, you have to identify the right technology and platform. Thanks to natural language processing (NLP) capabilities, chatbots can understand and respond to customer queries effectively. Cloud-based solutions and integration with existing systems will also enhance scalability and flexibility, making it easier for the chatbot to adapt to the evolving business requirements.

The Power of Conversational AI

In the previous chapter, we outlined the importance of assessing your readiness for AI before immersing your business in the deep end of it all. AI has such immense potential that you must fully understand why you need it before you invest in it. Beyond automation and machine learning, speech is one of the fundamental features of conversational AI that will make a big difference in your push for better customer engagement. Speech seems easy because you're basically training the chatbot how to communicate with people. It also happens to be the most important part of conversational AI, especially when looking at your customers' needs.

Conversational AI offers a multitude of benefits, and one prominent advantage is in optimal data collection. Data is at the heart of every modern business, so anything that can provide useful insight into various data points in your business will always be a welcome addition to it. The fact that chatbots conversationally interact with users allows them to extract valuable information in a structured format. This not only facilitates seamless communication but also helps your businesses gather rich insights about customer preferences, behavior, and feedback. Insight from this structured data could be useful when making important decisions about your business, for example, product offerings and marketing strategies that appeal to your customers.

Beyond insight, conversational AI can also help you make the business more efficient. Chatbots, for example, can handle repetitive tasks, answer frequently asked questions (FAQs), and assist with routine processes. This ultimately frees up resources so you can focus on more complex and strategic aspects of your business. This is also how you build a successful business around streamlined workflows, better response times, and increased overall operational efficiency.

You can also experience efficiency from a cost point of view, depending on the kind of AI you integrate into your business. By automating routine tasks and providing instant support, you reduce the need for a large customer support team, cutting labor costs. At the same time, the streamlined engagement with customers means that your team will only have to handle issues that the chatbot cannot, which in most cases are very few, thereby contributing to improved operational cost-effectiveness.

One of the most important things every business owner looks forward to is enhanced customer experiences. Your customers are your best and most effective brand ambassadors. You can even think of them as free marketing if you serve them well. The ability to provide real time, personalized interactions with your customers will create a positive and engaging customer journey. Besides, chatbots can be programmed to remember past interactions, understand user preferences, and offer tailored recommendations, creating a more seamless and customer-centric experience.

Whichever way you implement chatbots in your business, whether through your website, mobile apps, or messaging platforms, your customers benefit from all-round cross-platform support. This broadens your business reach, making your services more accessible to a diverse audience. This is how conversational AI improves accessibility to your audience. Accessibility is especially crucial in the modern business world because users expect convenient and immediate interactions with brands. More importantly, they expect genuine engagement.

Finally, conversational AI is built to allow you to personalize customers' experiences. This gives them some form of control in their interaction with your brand and, ultimately, supports your need for better user engagement. Chatbots make this possible by analyzing user data to provide personalized recommendations, product suggestions, and tailored content. This personalized approach makes interactions more meaningful and strengthens the connection customers have with your business, fostering loyalty and brand advocacy. That's why we mentioned earlier that your customers could be your best brand ambassadors!

If you look at the benefits your business stands to gain from conversational AI, you can only wonder why you didn't implement the strategy sooner. The diverse benefits collectively make it a valuable asset if you're hoping to stay competitive in the industry by adapting to evolving customer needs and preferences.

Building Your Chatbot

To harness the benefits we've outlined, here's a simple step-by-step guide to building and implementing a chatbot in your business.

- **Step 1: Define your purpose and objectives:** Clearly outline the reasons why you need the chatbot in the first place. Identify the specific objectives it is meant to achieve. This could be

anything from enhancing customer support to task automation or lead generation.
- **Step 2: Explore your audience:** Gain a deep understanding of the target audience for the chatbot. Analyze user demographics, preferences, and behaviors to tailor the chatbot's functionalities to meet their needs effectively.
- **Step 3: Build character into the model:** Infusing your chatbot with some character is a crucial step in creating a memorable user experience. Define a unique personality, tone, and communication style that aligns with your business brand or purpose. Design the character to the needs of your target audience, and maintain consistency in terms of language and demeanor. Whether it's a friendly assistant or a professional advisor, deliberate design choices such as vocabulary and humor help users connect on a personal level, making the interaction more enjoyable and memorable. You can give your chatbot a name.
- **Step 4: Identify an ideal platform and technology:** Choose a suitable platform and technology stack for your chatbot. Consider factors like integration capabilities, scalability, and the desired user interface. Common technologies include NLP, machine learning, and cloud-based solutions.
- **Step 5: Build conversational flow:** Conversational flow outlines possible user interactions and responses. Create a user-friendly and intuitive dialogue that aligns with the chatbot's objectives.

Incorporate branching scenarios to handle diverse user inputs, especially what can be escalated to your customer service team.
- **Step 6: System integration:** Ensure seamless integration with existing systems and databases used in your business. This is the kind of data your chatbot needs to provide accurate responses within the right context.
- **Step 7: Implementation:** Assuming that you're using NLP, for example, this is where you train the chatbot to recognize patterns, intent, and other crucial features of the language it's trained on, so it can engage your customers in a human-friendly manner.
- **Step 8: Testing:** Conduct rigorous testing to identify and address any issues in the chatbot's functionality. Test various scenarios and user inputs to ensure that the chatbot performs as expected. Iterate on the design based on user feedback and testing results.
- **Step 9: Compliance:** Make sure you implement security measures to protect user data and ensure compliance with relevant regulations and legislation in your jurisdiction. This is especially crucial if the chatbot handles sensitive information or operates within industries with specific compliance requirements.
- **Step 10: Training**: Use sample conversations and data to train the chatbot and improve its accuracy and effectiveness over time. Remember that training is continuous throughout to improve the

chatbot's performance and interaction with your customers.
- **Step 11: Deploy:** Once you're satisfied with the training outcome, deploy the chatbot across the desired platforms. This could be your website, apps, or any other platform where customers interact with your brand. After deployment, keep a close eye on the real-time performance, because there are always outliers you might not have captured through the training and development cycle. Apart from that, monitor how it performs against your desired KPI and user feedback. Note and address any issues promptly and make improvements as needed. An example log to help you collect this data is included in the AI accelerator at the end of this chapter. It can easily be operationalized into responses on a numeric scale.

Selecting the Right Tools: Quality Over Quantity

There are lots of chatbots on the market at the moment. A few effective examples include Manychat, Botsify, and WotNot. Each chatbot has unique features which you must consider to find the perfect fit for your business.

Remember, your ideal choice should be guided by your needs, goals, and vision for the business. Business owners are gradually coming to terms with the immense value of chatbots, hence the flood of chatbots in the market at the moment. Chatbots are effective in enhancing customer interactions and streamlining operations. To help you find an ideal fit, below are some factors you should keep in mind.

Simplicity

Top on your list should be ease of use. You wouldn't want a chatbot that's too complex for your customers or even your staff to work with. This would mean having to spend more on training or replacing the chatbot altogether—wasting precious time, money, and other resources. An ideal chatbot should empower users with a straightforward and intuitive interface, allowing them to quickly get started without needing extensive training. Look for tools that offer a drag-and-drop interface and prebuilt templates to facilitate a seamless setup process.

Ease of Integration

You can easily gauge the effectiveness of a chatbot by how seamlessly it integrates with the platforms and tools used in your business. Assess compatibility with your existing systems, databases, and communication channels. Integration ensures a cohesive workflow and maximizes its potential to enhance overall efficiency. Ease of integration loosely ties to the point of simplicity above. If it's too complex or demands a lot of configurations, you're better off trying something else.

Cost Consideration

This is something all business owners think about. Can you afford it? Being able to pay for it does not necessarily mean that you can afford it. For example, can you handle the training and maintenance costs? What about future upgrades? Budget considerations are crucial in any decision-making process, and selecting a chatbot is no exception. Evaluate the pricing structure to ensure you're looking at chatbots that fall within your budget. Beyond that, find out whether the chatbot offers scalable pricing options. This is important because it allows you to adapt and adjust the chatbot as your needs evolve.

Support

Put yourself in your customers' shoes. When you need help, you hope to get it as soon as possible. That's what you should get from the chatbot. Robust customer support will be crucial in successfully implementing and maintaining the chatbot. Choose a tool whose developers provide comprehensive support services, including responsive customer service, detailed documentation, and user forums where you can brainstorm emerging issues with other business owners. More importantly, access to timely support is necessary when you need to troubleshoot issues or optimize your chatbot's performance.

Customization

While chatbots are designed for mass markets, your business needs are different from other users. With this in mind, the right chatbot for your business should be customizable. Tailoring the chatbot to meet the unique requirements of your business is essential for its effectiveness. Look for a tool that offers extensive customization options, allowing you to define its workflow according to your specific needs. For example, this could include how you configure responses to certain keywords or knowing when to escalate issues to your customer support team.

Security and Compliance

Your chatbots will interact with customers, so there's a good chance they'll collect or process sensitive information. What security measures are built into the chatbot to protect your customer data? How do these measure up against local legislation? The last thing you want is a chatbot that will expose you to lawsuits, or risk your operating license, depending on the rules of engagement in your industry. Investigate the security features offered by the chatbot. For example, how do they handle data encryption? What security or authentication processes do they implement? More importantly, ensure that it aligns with industry-specific compliance standards to mitigate risks associated with data handling.

Scalability

Always think about scalability when choosing a chatbot for your business. After all, you do expect your business to grow, right? That's why you need a chatbot that can support your customer-centric needs. A scalable chatbot will save you on the cost of upgrades since it can comfortably adjust to the dynamic needs of your business as it grows.

The point here is to accommodate potential growth in user interactions and your business needs. A scalable solution enables your business to expand its chatbot capabilities seamlessly without facing limitations as user volumes increase. Discuss the chatbot infrastructure and capabilities with the developers to ensure it aligns with your long-term objectives.

Finally, choosing the right chatbot is one of the most important decisions you'll have to make. Considering the factors we outlined in this chapter, I believe you can now find an ideal solution for your business despite the overwhelming number of options available. It will take a comprehensive evaluation of factors to find the right one, but having considered these aspects, you can make an informed decision for your business. While nothing is perfect, an ideal chatbot will meet your current needs and position you for future success.

Now that you have a solid chatbot strategy in place, let's build on this in the next chapter, and explore ethical and secure approaches to customer interactions. Remember, at the end of the day, user privacy must always come first. This is how you build not just an effective chatbot into your business, but also a responsible one.

AI Accelerator

The feedback log below will help you gain insight into your customers' experience using your chatbots. Use this template to learn about what works for them, their frustrations, and how you can improve your chatbot strategy for better service delivery.

Feedback Interaction Log Template

Thank you for taking the time to provide feedback on your recent interaction with our chatbot. Your input is invaluable in helping us enhance and optimize the chatbot experience. Please use this form to record your feedback.

Date and Time of Interaction:

[Enter the date and time when you engaged with the chatbot]

User Details (Optional):

[Optional: Provide any relevant information about yourself that might impact the interaction]

---

1. What Went Well:

[Describe the positive aspects of your interaction with the chatbot. For example, did it understand your query accurately, provide helpful information, or guide you effectively?]

___

2. Areas of Improvement:

[Highlight any issues or areas where the chatbot could improve. This may include misunderstandings, incomplete responses, or any frustration you experienced during the interaction.]

___

3. Specific Feedback:

[Provide specific details on any phrases, questions, or responses that stood out to you, whether positively or negatively. This helps us pinpoint areas for improvement.]

___

4. Ease of Use:

[Comment on the overall ease of using the chatbot. Was the interface intuitive? Did you encounter any difficulties in navigating through the conversation?]

___

5. Suggestions for Enhancement:

[Share any suggestions you may have for improving the chatbot experience. This could include additional features, better language understanding, or any specific functionalities you believe would be beneficial.]

---

6. Overall Satisfaction:

[Rate your overall satisfaction with the chatbot interaction on a scale from 1 to 10 (1 being extremely dissatisfied, 10 being extremely satisfied).]

Additional Comments (Optional):

[Include any additional comments or thoughts you have about the chatbot interaction that may not have been covered in the previous sections.]

Thank you for your valuable feedback!

You can also check Smart Sheet for some examples of feedback forms you can use in your business.

www.smartsheet.com/feedback-forms-templates

CHAPTER 3: PRIVACY, SECURITY, AND ETHICS FOR CHATBOTS

> *Privacy means people know what they're signing up for, in plain language, and repeatedly. I believe people are smart. Some people want to share more than other people do. Ask them.*
>
> — STEVE JOBS

We're living in an age where data is one of the most valuable commodities. Think about it for a moment, your data is collected at various points of interaction, whether it's your browser, the apps on your phone, or even in offices that use biometric access controls. What do these entities do with your data? Let's say you open a website, and your browser settings flag it because of a security concern. Would you continue using that website? Unless you're willing to risk your data, you'd simply close the tab and find the information you seek elsewhere. That's the same experience that customers go through if they are unsure about their security when interacting with your chatbot.

You might build one of the most user-friendly chatbots ever into your business, but if your customers ever have a reason to doubt or have concerns about their privacy, security, or any ethical issue in their interaction, it could undermine everything you are trying to accomplish.

Data security is your obligation. You are your customers' first line of defense, so you must take this role seriously. Even though customers must still be diligent in their online habits and take proactive steps to protect their data, at the point of interaction with your business, their security becomes your objective. You could even be the target of litigation if your customers are exploited because you didn't have measures in place to protect them.

Data Privacy in Conversations

Given the inherent value of your customers' and your business's data, privacy and security must be woven into your AI strategy. Data privacy regulations govern the conduct of businesses and customers, especially in data management. Regulations generally provide guidelines on things like data security and encryption you must comply with. In the European Union, for example, there is the General Data Protection Regulation (GDPR).

GDPR is a comprehensive data protection and privacy regulation enforced by the EU on May 25, 2018, replacing the Data Protection Directive of 1995. The main objective of the GDPR is to give individuals greater control over their personal data and to harmonize data protection regulations across EU member states. Note that even though the GDPR is an EU directive, the guidelines often apply to businesses outside the EU.

There have been discussions and proposals to establish a comprehensive privacy framework at the federal level in the US, similar to the GDPR. Until that is put in place, however, you should always be guided by the local laws and legislation in your jurisdiction. Several states in the US have enacted their own privacy laws to address data protection concerns, for example, the California Consumer Privacy Act (CCPA), which is often considered the closest equivalent to the GDPR in the US.

While the landscape of privacy laws continues to evolve, the pillars will most certainly mirror those of the GDPR. Until such a time when distinct frameworks are in place, below are some important privacy and security lessons from the GDPR that you should take into consideration.

Understand Your Data

GDPR emphasizes the importance of knowing what personal data you collect, process, and store. It encourages you to maintain a comprehensive inventory of personal data. You must also document the categories of personal data you process, the purposes of collecting or handling it, and the legal basis for processing it. This makes it easier for you to understand why the data you collect or handle is valuable to your business.

Prioritize Data Use Cases

You must clearly define the purposes for which you collect and process personal data. For example, what's the legal basis for processing the data? It could be anything from consent, contract performance, legal obligations, business interests, or public interest. The point here is to make sure that your data handling activities align with the applicable legislation or regulations in your jurisdiction, and that your customers are informed about the purposes for which your business obtains their data.

Map Relevant Legal Requirements

The GDPR outlines various principles for the lawful and fair processing of personal data. In particular, it provides guidelines on transparency, purpose limitation, data minimization, accuracy, storage limitation, integrity, and confidentiality. Your responsibility to your customers is to ensure that your data handling efforts not only align with these guidelines but also comply with other legal requirements, for example, data subject rights, data protection impact assessments, and, where necessary, appoint a data protection officer to oversee the integrity of your data handling procedures.

Assess Your Data Stack

A data stack refers to the combination of tools, technologies, and processes used to manage and analyze data within your business. It typically includes various layers, including data storage, processing, analysis, and visualization. The components of a data stack can include databases, data warehouses, data processing frameworks, business intelligence tools, and visualization platforms.

The goal of a data stack is to provide a comprehensive and integrated solution for handling the data needs of your business, from collecting and storing raw data to extracting meaningful insights that can inform decision-making processes. The specific tools and technologies involved will depend on the requirements of your business, and the scale of data processing and analysis you need.

This guideline is about taking proactive steps to protect personal data. You must implement appropriate technical measures to ensure a level of security relevant to the possible risks involved in handling the particular data. If you have a data protection officer or data controller, their role is to ensure every step of your data processing lifecycle is streamlined following relevant laws and regulations—from data collection to storage and disposal.

Future-Proofing Your Data Solutions

While the emphasis here is on implementing data solutions that will stay relevant in the future, the underlying principle is accountability. You must regularly review and update your data processing practices. This can be done through regular audits, revisiting data protection impact assessments, and updating your privacy policies as needed. Accountability means adapting to changing times and continued compliance with relevant regulations and legislation, making it easier to address emerging privacy issues.

Ultimately, if you apply the principles above, you can easily build a holistic and proactive approach to data management that guarantees your customers' security and privacy at every point of interaction with your chatbots or any other AI solution you implement. The goal here, for your customers, is to guarantee them transparency, accountability, and a continuous commitment to compliance.

Early Version of Google's Gemini (formerly Bard), a "Pathological Liar"

Your employees will be the first point of contact with your AI. If they have a problem with it, rest assured that your customers will too. Such was Google's early experience with Gemini, its native chatbot. There was a time when Gemini (then called Bard) infamously provided dangerous feedback and advice to users. Internally, the safety teams had raised this issue, but Google continued the launch, disregarding their concerns. Google's reputation took a bit of a hit because of this, as they were seen as an enterprise driven solely by profit, with no regard for ethical or safety concerns (Vincent, 2023).

In an exclusive interview with Search Engine Journal, Yury Pinsky, Director of Product Management at Gemini, maintained that Google had gone to great lengths to address the earlier concerns about misinformation, sensitivity attributes, and unfair outcomes using the chatbot. More importantly, Google had measures in place to act swiftly on such issues (Southern, 2023).

Navigating Ethical Challenges in Chatbot Design

The last thing you want is to end up in a similar position as Google. Besides, Google has the financial muscle to weather the storm, something that most small businesses cannot. Reputational damage like this could significantly harm your business's bottom line. As you work toward building an efficient and successful business with AI, always remember that ethical considerations in chatbot design are necessary when creating responsible and user-friendly applications. Here are some important points to guide you through this.

Addressing the Risk of Bias

Bias in chatbots often stems from biased training data. Have your developers carefully curate and review training datasets to identify and eliminate biased patterns. This can help you avoid situations where your AI is essentially creating an efficient mess. To reduce bias, it's important to use diverse datasets that include a wide range of perspectives and experiences. This helps the chatbot provide more inclusive and balanced results. Since this is an evolving process, conduct regular audits of the chatbot's interactions to identify and rectify any emerging biases. This process makes it easier to refine the model and improve its fairness over time.

Sensitive Issues

This is another area where you must be careful, especially since the effect will be immediate on the customer's side. Clearly define guidelines for your chatbot's interactions with sensitive topics, such as mental health, politics, or personal issues. Establish what the chatbot can and cannot discuss to ensure responsible and respectful interactions. This might be a difficult one to handle since most business customers won't necessarily come online to discuss such matters with your chatbot. However, it's always wise to preempt such incidents and plan accordingly, rather than get ambushed and not know how to respond.

An ideal situation is a chatbot designed to respond with empathy and compassion when customers discuss sensitive topics. Provide appropriate resources, such as helplines or support links, when necessary. If the chatbot is specifically designed to handle personal or sensitive information, obtain explicit consent from users before engaging in such discussions. Clearly communicate how the data will be used and protected.

Transparency

You must be clear with your customers from the onset, and provide disclosures where necessary. For example, communicate your chatbot's capabilities and limitations. Customers should be aware that they are interacting with a machine and understand the scope of the chatbot's knowledge and abilities. This eliminates bias on the customer's side, so they are aware they are not dealing with a human who can empathize and understand the context of their engagement, but an AI model.

Do not build the chatbot to intentionally deceive or mislead customers about its identity. They should be aware that they are interacting with a chatbot, and the bot should not pretend to be a human. On top of this, inform your customers about any updates or improvements to the chatbot. If there are changes in its capabilities, let them know to manage expectations and maintain transparency.

At the end of the day, you can never preempt every response that your chatbot will give customers. Similarly, you cannot predict everything that customers will ask the chatbot. That being said, don't leave everything to chance. The smartest approach to navigating ethical concerns in chatbot design is to be proactive in the points we've discussed above.

Having explored the dynamics of ethical chatbot design, let's dive into some success stories. In the next chapter, we'll look at some real-world examples that will show you the potential of chatbots when done right.

AI Accelerator: SWOT Analysis

Use the sample checklist to assess the suitability of your AI, and customize it according to the industry requirements or your unique business needs.

Strengths

- **24/7 Availability:** Can your chatbot provide round-the-clock support to customers?
- **Cost Efficiency:** Will the integration lead to cost savings in HR?
- **Instant Response:** Can your chatbot provide quick and immediate responses to customer queries?
- **Data Collection:** Is your chatbot capable of collecting and utilizing valuable customer data?
- **Consistency:** Will your chatbot ensure consistent messaging and information delivery?
- List any existing assets or advantages your business already possesses that can make AI integration smoother.

_____

_____

Weaknesses

- **Limited Understanding:** Are there potential challenges in the chatbot understanding complex queries?
- **Initial Investment:** Have you considered the initial costs for technology implementation and training?
- **Dependence on Technology:** Do you have measures in place to address potential technical issues and service disruptions?
- **Lack of Empathy:** How will the chatbot handle situations that require emotional intelligence and empathy?
- **Continuous Maintenance:** Have you planned for ongoing updates and maintenance requirements?
- Are there areas where you don't collect data but should for AI to be effective? List them below

_____

_____

Opportunities

- **Enhanced Engagement:** Can the chatbot contribute to real-time engagement for an improved customer experience?
- **Sales Support:** Will the chatbot assist in sales processes, potentially increasing conversion rates?
- **Personalization:** Is there a plan to use the chatbot to deliver personalized recommendations based on customer data?
- **Integration Possibilities:** Are there opportunities for seamless integration with existing business systems?
- **Market Differentiation:** How can the integration of chatbots showcase innovation for a competitive edge?
- Pinpoint additional potential benefits and growth areas AI can bring to your business

_____

_____

Threats/Vulnerabilities

- **Security Concerns:** Have you addressed potential security and privacy issues associated with using chatbots?
- **Resistance to Technology:** How will you overcome potential customer resistance to chatbot interactions?
- **Technological Changes:** Is there a plan in place to stay updated with rapid technological advancements?
- **Negative Public Perception:** What measures will be taken to mitigate the risk of negative publicity due to chatbot glitches?
- **Regulatory Compliance:** Have you ensured that the chatbot integration complies with relevant data protection regulations?
- Recognize potential risks or external factors that could hinder the successful implementation of AI.

_____

_____

Action Steps

Based on the SWOT analysis, list specific steps you need to take. Whether it's attending an AI workshop, hiring an AI consultant, or initiating a pilot project, make sure these steps are concrete and actionable.

_____

_____

CHAPTER 4: THE CHATBOT CHRONICLES
SUCCESS IN THE LAND OF ALGORITHMS

> *We are stuck with technology when what we really want is just stuff that works.*
>
> — DOUGLAS ADAMS

The kind of difference that chatbots make in business growth is nothing short of astonishing. Take a look at just a few stats from Overthink Group that shed more light on this perspective (Nelson, 2017):

- **Anymail Finder** attributes 60% of its revenue to chatbot interaction, as 1 in 3 buyers used their Intercom chatbot system before making a purchase.
- **RapidMiner** replaced all lead capture forms with Drift chatbots, generating 4,000 leads and influencing 25% of its sales pipeline.
- **Bizbike** increased its lead conversion rate by 40%

in a few months and earned 20,000 leads in a year by replacing web-based forms with chatbots.

While the statistics paint an interesting picture of the input of chatbots in different settings, this is the tip of the iceberg. Chatbots are a way of life now, and they play a crucial role in supporting business growth in different sectors.

The Need for Chatbots

Chatbots can help businesses in different capacities. Given that businesses have unique needs, it's important to conduct a needs assessment to ensure that you are implementing chatbots where their impact will be immediate. Let's look at three common scenarios where implementing chatbots has proven to be an effective solution:

Managing Customer Queries

In situations where businesses experience a surge in customer inquiries, managing these manually can be challenging and time-consuming. Chatbots can efficiently handle numerous inquiries simultaneously, providing quick and consistent responses to common customer concerns. Through chatbots, it's easier to streamline the communication process, improving response times and overall customer satisfaction.

Overwhelmed Customer Service Representatives

This also comes down to the high volume of customer queries generally. During peak periods or sudden increases in customer inquiries, the capacity of human customer service representatives may become overwhelmed. With chatbots, you have an efficient first line of defense, addressing simple questions and FAQs. This frees up your team to focus on more complex issues requiring empathy, creativity, problem-solving skills, and other people skills. Besides, such a workload distribution helps prevent burnout among your team and ensures a more efficient allocation of resources.

Support Beyond Business Hours

In most cases, customer service is typically available during normal business hours, leaving customers short of immediate support in the evenings, weekends, or holidays. Since chatbots operate 24/7, they can provide continuous support and information to customers regardless of the time zone or the day of the week. This gives customers the guarantee of support at their convenience, and in the long run, it enhances their overall customer experience, strengthening their trust in your brand.

We've only covered three instances where chatbots can support business growth, to highlight the fact that the need to implement chatbots arises from the unique challenges each business faces from time to time. By leveraging chatbots, you can enhance efficiency, maintain consistent service levels, and improve customer satisfaction, ultimately contributing to a more robust and responsive customer support ecosystem. More importantly, you should remember that chatbots are not a solution to your problems but are a solution to helping you solve the problems efficiently.

Chatbot Implementation Process

For what needs are you trying to implement chatbot efficiency? That's the first question you should ask yourself before implementing chatbots in your business model. With this, you'll figure out the immediate problem, the specific functions or roles that you want the chatbot to perform, and finally, outline possible bottlenecks you'll encounter during the implementation process, and how to work around them. Let's shed more light on these fundamentals.

First, you'll need to conduct a thorough needs assessment to identify your pain points and how they could be addressed by a chatbot. You can get more information on this by analyzing customer inquiries, a review of your FAQs, and common issues that your customer support team raises from time to time. Set clear objectives outlining the specific functions and tasks the chatbot will perform to address the concerns raised.

Next, you have to identify the appropriate technology for implementation. Evaluate various chatbot platforms or technologies and assess their suitability for your needs. At this point, you'll be thinking about ease of integration with your existing systems, scalability, NLP capabilities, ease of customization, and so on.

Building on the tech, design an ideal conversation flow. The chatbot's conversation flow should be seamless and intuitive, making work easier for all users. Consider different user inputs and possible routes a typical conversation would take.

After that, integrate the chatbot with your business model. This is where you bring in your databases, customer relationship management (CRM) tools, or any other relevant system. The goal here is to allow the chatbot to access real-time data, for example, product availability or order status, to make sure that it can deliver accurate and up-to-date responses.

Test the system to identify and rectify any issues in the chatbot's functionality and responses. User feedback, both internally and externally, will help refine and improve the chatbot's performance.

Once you're satisfied with the outcome, you can fully deploy the chatbot across the entirety of your business model, or to relevant platforms. Use this on your company website, mobile apps, or social media channels. For broader accessibility, you might want to integrate the chatbot into messaging platforms like WhatsApp and Facebook Messenger.

Chatbot Functionality

What exactly should the chatbot do? Now, while this might seem redundant coming after the implementation process, there's a good reason for it. Even though you went through this before designing the implementation stage, it's still necessary to help you review whether the chatbot is meeting the very needs for which it was designed.

If you designed it to answer FAQs, has it been able to address them effectively? Is it providing detailed information about products or services, helping users make informed decisions? Has it been effective in streamlining order processing, for example, tracking, order placement, and other issues?

The most important part of this assessment is to address the human agent handover process. This is the escalation part. Most chatbots are programmed to recognize more complex queries or situations requiring human intervention, and seamlessly transfer the conversation to a customer service representative. How's that working out so far?

Addressing Integration Obstacles

The last step in this process is to address challenges encountered throughout the implementation process. This is important because it forms the foundation for reference material to guide future iterations.

Integration complexity is usually the first issue many businesses encounter. Difficulties in integrating existing systems and databases can be overcome by collaboration between your IT teams and third-party service providers. This is also the point where you discuss the accuracy of your NLP models. Achieving high accuracy in NLP could be a hurdle because it might take a while for the chatbot to understand and respond to a wide range of user inputs accurately. You can overcome this through regular feedback loops to continuously improve the chatbot's performance, addressing accuracy issues and refining conversation flows.

There's also the possible issue of user acceptance. Some users might initially resist or find it challenging to adapt to interacting with a chatbot, necessitating a robust change management and user education strategy. A workaround for this is clear communication and educational initiatives to help them understand the benefits of the chatbot and how to effectively interact with it.

Where chatbots are concerned, data security will always come up. You have to ensure the security of customer data and compliance with data protection regulations. With stringent security measures, for example, encryption and secure data storage, you can easily address data security concerns, effectively building robust security measures in the chatbot's design.

Each stage of the chatbot implementation process must be systematic and strategically designed to deliver an efficient solution to your needs.

Measurable Results

After integrating the chatbot, and if you aptly follow the results of your needs assessment, your business should experience a substantial boost in customer satisfaction scores. In most cases, surveys and feedback mechanisms should show an uptick in positive sentiments, reflecting the convenience and efficiency of chatbot-driven interactions.

One of the most tangible benefits should be a reduction in wait times for customer queries. The chatbot's ability to handle multiple inquiries simultaneously and provide swift responses alleviates the frustration associated with long wait times. This improvement could be reflected in your KPIs, with a notable decrease in average response and resolution times, indicating a more responsive and customer-centric support system.

Chatbots effectively guide users through product information, addressing queries promptly, and even facilitating order placements, resulting in a measurable conversion boost. Sales and lead generation metrics indicate a positive correlation between chatbot engagement and customer conversion rates.

Cost savings could also be another tangible benefit, with a reduction in human intervention for routine inquiries. By automating repetitive tasks and handling common queries, you reduce the workload for customer service representatives. This translates into cost savings associated with human resource allocation, allowing your team to focus on value-adding tasks.

In addition to the key metrics mentioned, your business could also realize improvements in other specific KPIs, for example, customer retention rates and engagement levels. The personalized and responsive interactions facilitated by the chatbot can also help to grow customer loyalty. Besides, the chatbot's ability to gather insights and preferences during interactions creates valuable data for targeted marketing strategies, further enhancing your overall customer engagement and long-term business relationships.

Post-Implementation Challenges

Despite the evident benefits, integration isn't always guaranteed to be a smooth process. After implementation, technical glitches can be a notable hurdle. You could have instances where the chatbot fails to understand certain inputs accurately, leading to frustration. (Yours not the chatbot.) These technical challenges require ongoing collaboration with your software development team to refine and optimize the chatbot's algorithms, ensuring a smoother user experience and higher accuracy in handling a diverse range of queries.

Another challenge you might encounter is customers who prefer human interaction for specific queries. While chatbots excel at routine inquiries, some users usually insist on the nuanced and empathetic support that human representatives offer. This is understandable, especially in complex or emotionally charged situations. Your goal is to strike a balance between automated responses and seamless handovers to your customer service team for personalized assistance. To achieve this, you must continuously monitor customer feedback and implement a dynamic approach to improve its ability to recognize situations that demand human intervention.

The need for continuous updates to the chatbot's knowledge base remains an ongoing opportunity. The business landscape is dynamic, and products, policies, and information evolve. The chatbot's effectiveness relies heavily on the accuracy and relevance of its knowledge base. Regular updates are necessary to keep up with relevant changes in products, services, and customer inquiries. To this end, you need a structured process for knowledge management and seamless integration with backend systems to ensure real-time information availability.

One of the biggest challenges you must overcome is user education. This is to help you address misconceptions and build trust in the chatbot. Some customers are skeptical about relying on AI for critical inquiries. Implementing educational initiatives to showcase the chatbot's capabilities, clarify its role, and highlight its benefits can help you overcome this problem, and foster greater acceptance among users.

Ongoing Management and Evolution

Chatbot management is an ongoing process that's crucial to its successful evolution and seamless integration into your business model. So, you should create a structured update schedule, with the chatbot's knowledge base reviewed and updated regularly. Information relevant to your products, services, and common customer queries must be routinely revised to reflect any changes in the business environment. This is to make sure that the chatbot remains a reliable source of information and continues to deliver accurate and up-to-date responses.

Conduct periodic reviews to assess overall effectiveness, with an emphasis on indicators such as response times, user satisfaction scores, and resolution rates. Customer feedback will also play a big role in this, to help you better understand user experiences and preferences, and use that to guide ongoing adjustments to the chatbot's functionality and conversation flows.

Looking to the future, if you are planning to upscale your business, you must also have a plan to upgrade the chatbot's capabilities. As customer interactions and business needs evolve, you have to enhance the chatbot's functionalities to meet new requirements. This may involve incorporating advanced NLP capabilities, expanding the range of supported languages, or integrating additional features, for example, voice recognition. The goal here is to stay ahead of technological advancements and ensure that your chatbot remains a cutting-edge tool for customer engagement.

The ongoing management of the chatbot should always align with your overall commitment to staying agile, responsive, and innovative in your business approach. This includes exploring options for integration with emerging technologies, such as machine learning algorithms, to continuously improve the chatbot's ability to understand and respond to user queries more intelligently.

AI Accelerator

Following our discussion on chatbot integration, reflect on the following questions and contemplate the applicability of the lessons learned to your business context:

Customer Needs Assessment

Reflect on your current customer service landscape. Are there patterns in customer inquiries that could benefit from automation through a chatbot? How well do you understand your customers' needs, and could a chatbot address specific pain points or enhance their overall experience?

_____

_____

Human–Automation Balance

Consider the balance between automated responses and human interaction in your customer service strategy. Are there scenarios where customers prefer or require human assistance? How can you strike the right balance to provide efficiency through automation while maintaining a personalized touch where needed?

_____

_____

The Need for Adaptability and Continuous Improvement

Evaluate your business approach to continuous improvement. How frequently do you update and refine your customer service tools and processes? Are there regular reviews and feedback loops to identify areas for enhancement, and how agile is your business in implementing changes based on insights and evolving customer needs?

_____

_____

Future-Proofing Your Business

Consider the future of customer service technology within your industry. Are there emerging technologies, beyond chatbots, that could revolutionize customer interactions? How can your business stay proactive in adopting and integrating new technologies to stay ahead of the curve and provide a competitive edge in customer service?

_____

_____

Growth Potential

Examine your business's scalability in terms of customer service. As your business grows, how well can your current customer service infrastructure accommodate increased volumes of inquiries? What strategies can you implement to scale your customer service capabilities efficiently, ensuring a seamless experience for both customers and your team?

_____

_____

We explored the successful integration and ongoing management of a chatbot in a business setting. The implementation involved meticulous planning, addressing immediate needs, and defining clear objectives, looking forward to tangible benefits like increased customer satisfaction, reduced wait times, and improved KPIs. Now that you've seen the transformative power of a chatbot in action, it's time to explore another AI marvel—personalization in marketing. Continue on to discover how hyperpersonalization can revolutionize your marketing strategies and catapult your business into a realm of unmatched customer engagement!

PART TWO

PERSONALIZATION IN MARKETING WITH AI

CHAPTER 5: CRAFTING A HYPERPERSONALIZED MARKETING STRATEGY

> *Many companies have forgotten they sell to actual people. Humans care about the entire experience, not just the marketing, or sales, or service. To really win in the modern age, you must solve for humans.*
>
> — DHARMESH SHAH

Did you know that the vast majority of consumers are more likely to shop with brands that provide relevant offers and recommendations?

This changes the dynamic of marketing. Mass marketing might still be effective, but not as much as it was back in the day. Instead, brands have moved on to hyperpersonalized marketing. This is the practice of tailoring marketing messages, content, and experiences to individual consumers based on their unique preferences, behaviors, and characteristics. It goes beyond the demographic and into the desire. AI is a major game-changer in this because it leverages advanced data analytics, AI, and machine learning to create highly individualized and relevant interactions.

In this concept, businesses collect and analyze data on each customer, including their browsing history, purchase patterns, demographics, and preferences. This data is then used to create targeted and highly personalized marketing campaigns that aim to resonate with the customer on a personal level. One might call it precision at the pulse of preference.

This approach usually involves real-time personalization, dynamic content adaptation, and the use of automation to deliver a seamless and highly relevant customer experience across a variety of channels, for example, websites, emails, social media, and mobile apps.

The Role of AI in Modern Marketing

Marketing, in general, has undergone significant transformations over the years, progressing from generic approaches to more personalized strategies and, ultimately, reaching the pinnacle of hyperpersonalization. This evolution has been driven by advancements in technology, data analytics, and the changing expectations of consumers.

In the early stages, brands employed generic strategies that targeted broad audiences without considering individual preferences or behaviors. Mass media, such as TV, radio, and print, were the primary channels for these campaigns. While effective to some extent, generic marketing has always struggled with precision and the ability to connect with diverse consumer segments at a personal level. (If your business is in this stage of marketing, it is past time to move on.)

Over time, aided by technological advancements, brands began to adopt personalized marketing strategies, relying on customer data to tailor messages and experiences. This shift created room for targeted advertising and content delivery using features like user demographics, location, and purchase history to deliver relevant interactions. (If your business has reached this stage of marketing, prepare to turn casual browsers into loyal customers by speaking their language.)

Hyperpersonalized marketing owes its success to an in-depth understanding of the customer's journey. This is about mapping and, at times, guiding the customer journey in real time. This includes identifying touchpoints, understanding their behaviors, and adapting the marketing strategy accordingly. Every touchpoint can be crafted to feel like a personal note passed in class. The goal here is to create a seamless and personalized experience throughout the customer's interactions with the brand.

All this is possible through data analytics and deep insight into user behavior and interaction on the respective platform. With access to advanced data analytics tools, marketers have access to in-depth customer interaction data that ultimately forms the foundation for creating highly personalized experiences.

What sets hyperpersonalization apart from other approaches is the sheer level of customization. Hyperpersonalization goes beyond demographic and historical data, incorporating real-time data and behavioral insights. It aims to understand the customer at the moment of engagement, providing a more immediate and contextually relevant experience. In other words, done well it captures the fine art of individual attention.

This is all about understanding and responding to a customer's unique preferences, behaviors, and context in real-time. This level of customization requires a deeper understanding of each customer's journey and a more dynamic and adaptive approach, and that's where the power of AI reigns supreme.

Hyperpersonalized Marketing in Everyday Life

You interact with lots of hyperpersonalized marketing content almost every day. Good examples of this include Netflix and Amazon, which leverage this concept for enhanced user experiences. This is how they do it.

Netflix

Netflix employs a robust recommendation engine that analyzes viewing history, ratings, and user preferences to suggest personalized movie and TV show recommendations. It also uses machine learning algorithms to continuously improve these recommendations.

Over time, Netflix dynamically personalizes the artwork, titles, and descriptions of content based on your viewing habits. This is how it tailors the interface to your taste, increasing the likelihood of engagement.

The autoplay feature starts the next episode in a series automatically. Similarly, its "skip intro" feature recognizes that some people prefer to skip the opening credits.

Amazon

Amazon uses sophisticated algorithms to analyze customers' browsing and purchase history. This data is used to generate personalized product recommendations, prominently displayed on the homepage and throughout the website.

You might have realized that Amazon adjusts prices dynamically based on various factors, including your historical activity on its website, demand fluctuations, and competitor pricing. It will also send you targeted email campaigns featuring product recommendations, special offers, and personalized content based on your preferences and past activity on its website.

Both Amazon and Netflix leverage vast amounts of data and advanced algorithms to provide a highly personalized and seamless experience for their users, which goes a long way in improving customer loyalty and satisfaction.

The Role of AI in Your Marketing Strategy

So, AI has become a monster tool in marketing, with tangible benefits like enhanced efficiency, precision, and personalization. But it's not just for the giants like Amazon, there is something for everyone in AI marketing. Here's some insight into how you can use AI to transform your marketing strategy.

Content Generation and Moderation

Looking at the array of AI tools currently available on the market, you have quite the arsenal to create engaging and personalized content by analyzing user preferences and trends. This not only saves time but also ensures that the content resonates with the target audience.

AI can also analyze and moderate user-generated content on digital platforms, ensuring compliance with guidelines and preventing the dissemination of inappropriate content. This is crucial for maintaining a positive brand image and user experience.

Ad Targeting and Analysis

There are lots of AI algorithms that can analyze huge amounts of user data to identify patterns and preferences, making it easier for you to target specific demographics with personalized ads. This approach makes your marketing effort more effective and relevant, leading to higher conversion rates. On top of that, you can also use tools like

Google Analytics, Adroll, Revealbot, and Mailchimp to generate useful insights into the performance of various ad campaigns in real-time.

Social Media Listening and Brand Awareness

What are people saying about your company? There are many AI tools to monitor social media platforms for mentions of your brand, product, or industry-related keywords. With this analysis, you can easily understand customer sentiment, identify useful trends you can jump on, and respond promptly to customer feedback or address their concerns. Through AI, it's easier to grow your brand awareness by automating social media posting schedules, analyzing engagement data, and recommending strategies to increase your visibility and influence on social platforms.

Data Analysis

AI excels at processing and analyzing large volumes of data quickly and accurately. It can uncover insights and trends that may be harder or take considerably longer for humans to identify. This is a good boost to your data-driven decision-making needs, helping your team refine strategies, optimize campaigns, and improve overall performance.

The role of AI in your marketing strategy is, therefore, quite an important one, as it can give you a competitive advantage by automating processes, improving your targeting precision, and supporting data-driven decision-making.

Implementing AI for Personalized Customer Journeys

Customer segmentation through AI means leveraging AI algorithms to categorize customers based on various factors such as behavior, interests, and purchase history. This segmentation makes it easier for you to tailor your strategies to different customer groups, providing more personalized and relevant experiences. Here's how AI can help with this:

- AI can analyze customer behavior across different points of interaction, for example, social media engagement and email responses, identifying patterns and preferences. From this, AI will easily segment customers according to their behavior, allowing you to send targeted content and offers that match their preferences.
- AI can also process data based on user preferences, for example, tracking the content they engage with, products they view, and topics they show interest in. This approach helps marketers create targeted campaigns that resonate with specific segments of their audience.

Analyzing historical purchase data is a crucial aspect of customer segmentation. Your algorithms monitor trends, frequency of purchases, product preferences, and other features relevant to customer purchase activity. From this information, you can create customer segments like high-value customers, frequent buyers, or those who have lapsed in their purchases, giving you precision with effective and personalized marketing strategies.

Thanks to AI, you can also implement dynamic content creation into your marketing strategy, helping you create personalized content for each consumer based on their characteristics, preferences, and behaviors. Here's how to achieve this:

- **Personalized recommendations:** Algorithms analyze customer data and based on this information, you get useful insight to create personalized product or content recommendations on websites, emails, or other marketing channels, enhancing the likelihood of engagement and conversion.
- **Tailored messaging:** This is where you create unique messages that appeal to a specific audience. The dynamic approach to this involves altering certain content elements, for example, images, headlines, or calls to action, so that you create a unique, personalized, and engaging experience.
- **Individualized emails:** In email marketing, the goal is to personalize content like product recommendations, promotions, or any other content to match the recipient's interests to improve open and click-through rates.

Given the kind of data AI can access and analyze, the data-driven insights go a long way in helping you create dynamic and customizable content. The level of automation and ability to synthesize vast amounts of data saves time and resources compared to manual content curation. This is a continuous process, as algorithms perpetually learn and adapt based on user interactions. The good news here is that your content will always be relevant and adaptable to current market trends. And don't forget AI can facilitate consistent personalization across various channels, for example, websites, mobile apps, email, and social media. This gives you a unified and coherent user experience wherever your brand lives online.

There are many ways to introduce dynamic content creation into your marketing approach, and many more will emerge in the future. The most important point here is to recognize and understand the power of AI in delivering highly targeted and relevant experiences for your customers.

Tool Selection: Balancing Cost and Capability

We've recently witnessed a significant upsurge in the use of AI tools. The proliferation of AI tools in marketing is driven by the need for more efficient and effective strategies to navigate the complexities of modern consumer behavior and the digital ecosystem. Here are some common tools you might have come across already:

- **Sprout Social:** A social media management platform that offers social listening, analytics, scheduling, and engagement tools for businesses to manage their social media presence effectively.

- **Jasper:** An AI-powered analytics and business intelligence platform with advanced analytics, data visualization, and reporting capabilities to help businesses make smarter data-driven decisions.
- **Writer:** AI writing assistant that can help you create clear and concise content by suggesting improvements in grammar, style, and tone. It is particularly useful for content creation and editing.
- **Surfer SEO:** A search engine optimization (SEO) tool you can use to analyze and optimize content for search engines. It also provides insights and suggestions for improving your on-page SEO.
- **Grammarly:** One of the best writing and grammar assistants in the game. Grammarly can help you create error-free content by offering suggestions for grammar, spelling, and punctuation.
- **Hemingway Editor:** This is a writing-improvement tool created to help you improve the readability of your content. Hemingway highlights complex sentences, suggesting simpler alternatives, and providing a readability score.
- **Seventh Sense:** An email marketing optimization tool that uses AI to analyze data and determine the optimal times to send emails. This makes it easier for you to improve engagement and increase the likelihood of responses from your target audience.
- **Optimove:** An AI-driven CRM and marketing optimization tool that helps you analyze customer data, predict behavior, and automate personalized marketing campaigns for customer retention and loyalty.

- **Tidio:** This is an AI-powered chatbot and live chat platform that helps you improve user engagement on your website through AI-driven chatbots, providing instant responses and assistance where necessary.

The list above is just the tip of the iceberg. There are lots more on the market, and many others are still being developed, serving various business needs. With marketers increasingly turning to these tools to gain insights, automate routine tasks, and deliver more personalized and targeted campaigns, it's important to understand what your immediate needs are and then use that information to shortlist relevant tools that can effectively help you achieve your objectives.

AI Accelerator

This worksheet gives you a structured way of estimating and analyzing the costs associated with implementing AI tools in marketing. Adjust the categories and details according to your specific requirements and circumstances.

Objective and Scope

Define your goals and objectives for this implementation, and the scope, for example, personalized content, customer segmentation, predictive analysis, and so on.

_____

_____

Recommended Tools and Technologies

List the specific AI tools and technologies you plan to implement.

_____

_____

Research and estimate the costs associated with each tool.

Technology	Vendor Name	Cost	Implementation Timeline and Notes
Tool 1		$	
Tool 2		$	
Tool 3		$	

Data Integration

List the data sources that AI tools will utilize.

_____

_____

Estimate the costs for integrating and cleaning data. You can get more insight into this by researching what your competitors or relevant businesses in your niche are doing.

Data Source	Integration Cost	Data Cleaning Cost	Implementation Timeline and Notes
Source 1	$	$	
Source 2	$	$	
Source 3	$	$	

Training and Skills Development

Assess the need for training your team in AI-related skills.

_____

_____

Estimate training costs and allocate time for skill development.

Training Program	Cost	Timeline	Implementation Timeline and Notes
AI Basics Workshop	$		
Tool-Specific Training	$		
Skills Development	$		

Implementation and Integration

Estimate the costs associated with implementing and integrating AI tools.

Cost	Timeline	Implementation Timeline and Notes
$		
$		

Maintenance and Support

Consider the ongoing maintenance and support costs for AI tools.

Activity	Cost	Timeline	Implementation Timeline and Notes
Maintenance	$		
Support	$		

Total Estimated Cost

Sum up all the estimated costs from the above sections.

Task	Cost
AI Tools	$
Data Integration	$
Training	$
Implementation	$
Maintenance	$
Total Estimated Cost	$

CHAPTER 6: ETHICS AND SECURITY IN AI-DRIVEN MARKETING

> *Cancel culture is a real thing. Your digital footprint is your legacy, so think before you post.*
>
> — GERMANY KENT

Ethics and security play an important role in shaping not just the success of your marketing campaigns but also the trust and credibility of your business. As we continue to interact with AI in the era of data-driven decision-making, it becomes imperative to understand the ethical considerations and security challenges you might encounter from time to time.

We talk about ethical considerations all the time. How do you treat your employees, your customers, and so on? AI takes things a notch higher since it can automatically perpetuate biases that could hurt your business. This is why ethics is the cornerstone of establishing lasting relationships with consumers. It is about integrity and mutual respect.

The power of AI to analyze vast amounts of data and predict consumer behavior is quite a transformative phenomenon. But it brings with it the responsibility to ensure that these insights are employed reasonably and respectably. Respect for privacy, transparency in data usage, and avoiding discriminatory practices are ethical and necessary to build and maintain customer trust. Remember that your competitors are equally using AI, so the difference between you and them is whoever can get the most value from their integration while at the same time setting themselves as a beacon of responsible AI use in an increasingly interconnected world.

Security, on the other hand, protects the very foundation of AI-driven marketing. The sensitivity and abundance of data make the marketing ecosystem susceptible to cyber threats. Think about it for a moment, every other company, brand, product, or service you use today collects some data about you. Why do they need this data? How do they use it? Who else has access to that data, and for those who sell your data, to whom?

Data security is a hot topic in the business world today; and for a good reason. From protecting customer information to preventing breaches, the need for a robust security framework is nonnegotiable. Your AI model is only as reliable as the security measures you put in place, and any compromise not only jeopardizes the sensitive information within your control but also erodes the confidence of your clients and customers.

In essence, weaving ethics and security into the fabric of your AI-driven marketing efforts is not just about adhering to industry best practices, but it is a strategic step that every business owner must embrace. When you do this, you will ensure compliance with evolving regulations and pave the way for a sustainable and responsible future for AI in marketing. By design, AI is built to learn in perpetuity, so why not give it the best foundation? The goal here is to optimize your AI model for desirable results and be the champion of values that will shape the future of marketing.

Protecting Customer Data in Marketing Campaigns

Threats to data security are at an unprecedented level, posing significant challenges to individuals, businesses, and even governments. Addressing these threats requires a multifaceted approach, including continuous cybersecurity awareness training, robust encryption measures, regular system updates and patches, and a proactive cybersecurity strategy that anticipates and mitigates potential risks. As technology continues to advance, you have to stay vigilant and adaptive to protect you and your customers' information. The interesting thing about cybersecurity today is that the imminent risk can be attributed to several factors, most of which we interact with every day.

Cybercriminals have become increasingly sophisticated, utilizing advanced approaches such as ransomware, phishing, and malware to exploit vulnerabilities in systems. These attacks are often difficult to detect and can lead to unauthorized access, data theft, or complete system compromise.

The Internet of Things (IoT) has brought about a surge in interconnected devices, from smart home gadgets to industrial machinery. Each connected device represents a potential entry point for cyber threats, and many IoT devices may have weak security measures or lack regular updates, making them susceptible to exploitation.

The widespread adoption of cloud computing services introduces new challenges in terms of data security. While cloud providers invest heavily in security measures, there's always the risk of being vulnerable to misconfiguration, inadequate access controls, or insecure application programming interfaces (APIs), which ultimately expose your sensitive data to unauthorized users.

With more communication over digital channels, the risk of data interception and eavesdropping increases. Cybercriminals are always looking to exploit weak encryption protocols or target unsecured communication channels to intercept and collect sensitive information during transmission, which leaves your business and customers exposed.

How do criminals get in?

A common tactic these days is social engineering. There are different ways to go about this, but it all comes down to criminals trying to persuade or coerce you or someone with access to your network, to allow them into your system. At times, they don't even need to get into the system—all they have to do is convince you to share some privileged information with them, usually by impersonating a trusted entity, for example, your internet service provider.

One of the complexities of today's cyber threats is their global nature, allowing potential attacks from anywhere. This highlights the importance of robust cybersecurity measures and being aware of your surroundings. Staying compliant with regulations like GDPR and CCPA not only helps avoid legal issues but also strengthens your reputation by demonstrating a commitment to data protection and customer privacy.

Compliance with these regulations is not only essential for your business but also offers an opportunity to excel in it. By adhering to guidelines that demand rigorous handling of personal data, emphasizing transparency and consumer rights, your business demonstrates its commitment to ethical practices. Investing in the necessary processes and training ensures your team is well-equipped to uphold these standards. It positions your company as a leader in integrity and customer care, one that customers can trust with their data.

Threat Mitigation Strategies

In light of these risks, it makes sense to take precautionary measures and be proactive in protecting not just customer data, but any type of data that happens to pass through your hands. Let's look at some useful strategies to mitigate these threats.

Assess Your Data Risks

Before you set up your marketing campaigns, you need to conduct an assessment of potential data risks. Begin by identifying the types of customer data in your possession and conducting a thorough analysis of the relevant vulnerabilities. There are different risk assessment frameworks that you can use for this. You employ penetration testing tools to simulate potential security breaches. This proactive approach allows you to identify weak points in your data infrastructure, giving you a good starting point for developing a targeted security strategy. Regularly reassess and adapt your risk assessment as your marketing campaigns evolve, because legislation around AI will also continue to change. This is to ensure that you are always prepared, especially in light of dynamic emerging threats to AI integration in business settings.

Encrypt Your Data

Data encryption stands as a formidable defense against potential data breaches. Implement robust encryption methods to protect customer data both during transmission and storage. Make sure you are using encryption tools that adhere to industry standards, ensuring the confidentiality and integrity of the information in your possession.

By encrypting sensitive data even in the event of unauthorized access, the information becomes worthless to hackers, because they cannot make sense of it without the appropriate decryption protocols. This essential layer of security protects your customers' privacy and makes sure that your business aligns with applicable regulatory requirements in your jurisdiction.

Control Your Data Access

I cannot overstate the need to control data access, particularly within the context of AI use in marketing campaigns. You must implement stringent access controls to limit data access exclusively to authorized persons. For this reason, you can use identity and access management tools to define and manage user privileges, ensuring that personnel only have access to the data necessary for their roles. Regularly audit and update access permissions to align with evolving responsibilities within your organization. By adopting the principle of least privilege, you reduce the risk of unauthorized data access and enhance the overall security of your marketing efforts.

Back Up Your Data

A robust data backup strategy is a must-have when mitigating the potential risk of data loss or corruption in your business. Establish a systematic backup system that regularly and securely stores customer data. Cloud-based backup solutions offer scalability and accessibility, allowing for efficient backup processes. Additionally, you might want to consider implementing automated backup procedures to streamline this process and minimize the risk of oversight.

Go beyond cloud backups and have some copies of customer data physically stored in secure locations off-site. This gives you a fail-safe that can come in handy if there is an extensive data breach that forces you to start from scratch. The goal here goes beyond preserving the integrity of your marketing initiatives, but also to ensure that your business is not crippled in the event of an extensive malicious exploit.

Educate Your Data Users

Human error is always a key factor in data security. Regular training sessions are necessary if you need to cultivate a culture of awareness and responsibility among your employees. Make a point to educate them on data security best practices, including the ability to recognize and prevent phishing attempts.

Remind them of the need to adhere to established security protocols and instill a sense of responsibility in protecting customer data. If you can create a culture of vigilance in your business, you empower your team to be proactive in identifying and addressing potential security threats. This ultimately helps in building resilient defenses against data breaches.

The Need for Regular Security Audits and Updates

Think of the digital infrastructure in your business as a fortress, standing tall against threats that are always evolving. Periodic security audits are like fortifying the walls of your castle, checking for potential weaknesses, and reinforcing the defenses around your valuable data. Security audits are a proactive approach, making it easier for you to identify vulnerabilities before they can be exploited by malicious actors. By assessing the effectiveness of your existing security protocols and scrutinizing potential weak points, these audits can help you preempt cyber threats. On top of that, they give you valuable insights into the evolving tactics that criminals use and help you stay a step ahead in protecting your business data.

It's advisable to update your security infrastructure for optimal performance regularly. Software vulnerabilities have always been a common entry point for criminals, especially since they understand that many business owners barely pay attention to security patches and fixes, or update their programs regularly.

The good news is that developers continually release patches to address such weaknesses, so all you have to do is regularly update your software solutions to make sure that your systems are equipped with the latest defenses, closing potential entry points for hackers. It's also in your best interest to embrace a culture of proactive maintenance, to not only enhance security but also demonstrate a commitment to cybersecurity.

Why Do Security Audits Regularly?

Here are some reasons why you should always conduct regular security audits.

Identifying Vulnerabilities

Regular security updates play an important role in identifying and addressing vulnerabilities within your security infrastructure. Cyber threats continually evolve, and proactive updates will help you get ahead of potential exploits. By regularly scrutinizing and fortifying your security protocols, you can easily thwart emerging threats and keep your business safe. This ongoing process of identifying vulnerabilities and mitigating them is fundamental in protecting your sensitive data from falling into the wrong hands.

The Need for Compliance

As the digital space evolves, so do the data protection regulations, especially where AI and data are concerned. With regulations like the GDPR in place, regular audits help you ensure you're running a compliant business and implement adequate measures to protect customer data. Compliance isn't just about avoiding legal repercussions; it's a testament to your dedication to upholding ethical standards and protecting the privacy of your customers.

Protecting Your Reputation

Reputation is such a fragile commodity in the world today. This explains the thriving reputation management industry. Many companies have struggled when their reputations came into question in the aftermath of data breaches or other security incidents that they were unable to handle appropriately.

With regular security updates, you're taking a proactive approach against potential breaches that could compromise customer trust. Robust security infrastructure is a sign of your commitment to protecting the confidentiality and integrity of the data you handle. This goes beyond protecting sensitive information, but also protecting your reputation in the eyes of your customers.

Remember that in the business world today, perceptions go a long way, and the last thing you want is for your customers to harbor concerns about your data protection measures. You want to stand out as one who takes data protection seriously, instilling a sense of trust and confidence in your customers. Trust is hard-earned and easily lost, making regular security updates an invaluable investment in preserving your business's credibility.

Saving Money

While it may seem counterintuitive, regular security updates contribute to significant cost savings in the long run. The financial fallout from a data breach—I am talking about the legal fees, regulatory fines, and efforts in damage control—far exceeds the investment in proactive security measures. Updates help you in closing potential vulnerabilities before they can be exploited, preventing costly incidents that could harm your business financially.

In essence, you need to look at regular security updates as a cost-saving measure. This underscores their role in protecting user data and your business's financial health. Think of data security as an investment that pays dividends by mitigating the substantial financial risks that could come about if your business were ever under attack from cyber threats.

Case Studies

Let's look at two good examples that highlight the need for proper security audits.

Case 1: Target

In 2013, retail chain Target fell victim to a high-profile data breach during the holiday shopping season. The attackers gained access to Target's network through a third-party HVAC contractor, exploiting weaknesses in the company's security infrastructure. The breach compromised credit and debit card information of approximately 40 million customers. The hackers also managed to get access to personal information such as names, addresses, and phone numbers of an additional 70 million individuals.

The immediate consequence for customers was the risk of unauthorized transactions and potential identity theft.

Target faced significant financial losses, including the costs associated with investigating and mitigating the breach, providing credit monitoring services for affected customers, and dealing with a decline in sales and customer trust.

The incident had lasting implications on Target's reputation, emphasizing the importance of cybersecurity in the retail sector. The fallout from the Target breach also prompted increased scrutiny of the security practices of other businesses, leading to a heightened awareness of the potential consequences of failing to protect customer data in the face of sophisticated cyber threats.

Case 2: Equifax

Equifax, one of the largest credit reporting agencies, experienced a massive data breach that had profound consequences in 2017. The breach exposed the sensitive personal information of approximately 147 million individuals, including names, Social Security numbers, birthdates, addresses, and in some cases, driver's license numbers. The attackers exploited a vulnerability in Equifax's website software, allowing them to gain unauthorized access to a vast repository of consumer data.

The impact on individuals was severe, as the compromised data provided the hackers with the means to commit identity theft, fraud, and other malicious activities. The fallout from the Equifax breach extended to the financial industry, with increased risks of fraudulent financial transactions and compromised credit scores for the affected individuals. The incident also led to widespread public outrage and eroded trust in Equifax's ability to protect sensitive information. In the aftermath, Equifax faced numerous lawsuits, regulatory investigations, and a significant financial toll, highlighting the broader implications of a data breach on both individuals and the company's overall reputation.

Ethical Considerations in Personalization

When we talk about personalization, the goal is to offer users a uniquely curated experience that aligns with their tastes, preferences, and needs. From unique product recommendations to content suggestions, this customized approach aims to make online interactions more relevant to each user, and efficient. Yet, as we tread this path, it's crucial to recognize and respect the boundaries of their privacy. Your marketing approach becomes intrusive when personalization becomes too invasive, to a point where your customers feel like their every move is being monitored.

The ethical considerations in personalization revolve around finding that sweet spot where customization adds value to your customers without compromising their privacy. You must be transparent about the data you collect and how it's used, providing users with clear choices and control over their personal information. Striking this balance not only preserves user trust but also ensures that personalization remains a tool for enhancing user experiences rather than a source of discomfort or mistrust.

Mitigating Bias in AI

As you work toward towing that line between personalization and ethical considerations when you integrate AI into your marketing efforts, it's important to also understand how to ensure AI doesn't reinforce societal biases or stereotypes. This is one of the biggest concerns facing many businesses that have integrated AI into their operations. Let's explore some simple approaches you can use to mitigate bias in AI.

Diverse and Representative Data

Consider data as the foundation of AI's knowledge. If this foundation is skewed, the entire structure becomes inherently biased. To address this, you need to actively seek out and incorporate diverse datasets that represent various demographics, perspectives, and experiences into your AI model. This is a conversation you should have with the developers behind the AI tools you are interested in. They should explain to you the kind of datasets used to train the AI model, and more importantly, potential biases you might encounter.

By including a wide range of voices, your AI gains a more comprehensive understanding of the world. This inclusivity helps mitigate the risk of reinforcing existing biases or inadvertently sidelining certain groups. It's about ensuring that AI learns from a rich set of data, avoiding the pitfalls of narrow, homogeneous datasets that might perpetuate unfortunate stereotypes.

If you can recall the case of Amazon's AI that perpetuated biases in recruitment, or Google's earlier version of Gemini that was labeled a pathological liar, Amazon and Google have the resources to weather the storm. They can easily pull their AI offline and have a team of developers working round the clock to fix the problem, pay their public relations experts to manage the narrative online, and so on. Your business, however, might not be able to do all that.

This is why you should always take proactive measures and engage all the relevant stakeholders in the AI chain, to ensure that you understand what you are integrating into your business, and more importantly, what to be on the lookout for. Your marketing efforts are about connecting with your customers. Make this as genuine as possible and your customers will love you for it.

Rigorous Testing and Evaluation

Just as we assess a student's performance through exams and evaluations, AI algorithms need rigorous testing protocols. This involves scrutinizing the outcomes and decisions made by AI for any signs of bias. Testing must go beyond traditional metrics to include comprehensive evaluations that consider the impact on different demographic groups.

By implementing a robust evaluation framework, the goal is to create a system of checks and balances that ensures that any unintended biases or unfair outcomes are identified and addressed promptly. Remember that testing is not just a one-time task. It is an ongoing process that evolves with the life cycle of your AI. Testing allows you better insight into the nature of biases your AI model might present.

Apart from that, you can also join discussion groups online to learn more about what other businesses that have implemented the same AI model are dealing with in their operations. The goal here is to integrate an AI model into your business that can adapt to new challenges without the risk of biases that may arise over time. Besides, regular evaluations help you mitigate the risk of accountability, reinforcing your commitment to fairness and equity.

Transparent and Explainable Algorithms

How do we trust AI to do the right thing? That's only possible if its decision-making process is transparent and explainable. This transparency allows us to understand why AI arrives at a particular decision, making it easier to identify and rectify any biases that might have influenced its judgment. Utilizing explainable algorithms not only fosters accountability but also empowers developers and users to scrutinize the decision-making mechanisms of AI systems. This transparency can protect your business against the opaque reinforcement of biases, as it encourages an open dialogue about the ethical implications of AI decisions. Once again, this is a conversation you need to have with the AI developers before you integrate their model into your business, so you know what you are signing up for.

Continuous Monitoring and Adaptation

AI models are designed to continuously learn and adapt. You should be keen on the kind of results you're getting from your AI, to catch any biases that might emerge as the AI interacts with new data or evolves in a changing environment. Regular check-ins ensure that the AI remains aligned with ethical standards, and adjustments can be made promptly if any biases are detected.

This dynamic approach acknowledges the fact that our perspectives and norms are fluid, particularly when it comes to meeting customer needs, tastes, and preferences, which is the core of marketing. To that effect, the AI model you've integrated into your business model must have the capacity to not only learn but also adapt accordingly over time.

By embracing a model of continuous improvement, you're creating a system that evolves responsibly, staying ahead of the risk of possible biases that might arise in the future, and making sure that AI has a positive influence on your marketing efforts. Besides, this adaptability is a key component of building trustworthy and unbiased AI models, not just for your business but also for the greater marketing field.

Inclusive Development Teams

Picture yourself in a classroom where only one type of student has a say in what's being taught—it would lack diversity and everyone else would miss out on valuable perspectives. Similarly, to avoid biases in AI, it's crucial to have inclusive development teams. Bringing together individuals with diverse backgrounds, experiences, and perspectives ensures a more comprehensive understanding of potential biases.

Inclusive teams create an environment where challenging assumptions and questioning the status quo become integral to the development process. This inclusivity not only helps in identifying and addressing biases but also enriches the overall AI development process, leading to more robust, ethical, and unbiased AI. By incorporating a variety of viewpoints, inclusive development teams contribute to the creation of AI that reflects the diversity and values of the societies it serves.

Now, this is a difficult one to approach, particularly because the diversity we're talking about targets the AI developers who create the AI. That being said, you can simply build an inclusive marketing team. Remember that even though AI is effective, it can never be a replacement for your people. Therefore, model your AI team around inclusivity. This makes it easier for you to identify biases that might not have been captured by the developers, and take appropriate action to mitigate the challenges that might arise from those biases.

Ethical Implications of Data Sourcing

Data ethics is essentially the moral code governing the collection, storage, analysis, and use of data. It's like the unwritten rules that keep things fair and square in the digital world. Picture this: You wouldn't want someone digging through your diary without permission, right? Similarly, data ethics is about treating people's information with respect and being transparent about how you're handling it.

Now, think of it as a two-way street. On one side, there's the responsibility of those collecting and crunching the data—making sure it's done ethically, without stepping on anyone's toes or compromising privacy. On the other side, it's about empowering individuals to know what's happening with their data and giving them a say in how it's used. It's all about finding that place where innovation and privacy coexist.

In a nutshell, data ethics is the moral compass that keeps our digital activities in check. It's about respecting privacy, being transparent, and making sure everyone involved—from the data collectors to the data subjects—is treated fairly. With that in mind, here are some core principles to guide you in your data approaches.

Ownership

Ethically sourcing data means acknowledging and respecting the fact that data belongs to individuals or entities. It's quite simple: Do not use AI to obtain customer data in a manner that would raise concerns. If you are collecting user data, let them know what data you need and why you need it. More importantly, allow them to opt out of sharing certain data with you. Just like you wouldn't barge into someone's backyard uninvited, ethical data sourcing is about obtaining data with permission and understanding the responsibility that comes with handling it.

Transparency

The goal of ethical data sourcing is to be open and honest about what data is being collected, how it's being used, and who's doing the collecting. It's about avoiding the murky waters of hidden agendas and ensuring that everyone involved understands the journey their data is taking from the moment they entrust you with it.

Privacy

Respecting privacy in data sourcing means protecting personal information and avoiding any activities that might be considered intrusive. Just as you wouldn't want someone peeking through your curtains, ethical data sourcing means protecting the privacy of your customers' data and ensuring their data doesn't end up where it shouldn't.

Many business owners simply ask for user data, but never take a moment to consider the kind of responsibility that comes with it. If they are not able to protect their customers' data and use it only for the right reasons, they have no business asking for it in the first place. The reason for this is that data is one of the most valuable commodities in the business world at the moment, and access from the wrong people could have far-reaching effects, both for the business and for the users who share it with them.

Intent

When it comes to ethical data sourcing, you must always have good intentions and ensure that data is collected for legitimate and fair purposes. If you need customer data for marketing purposes, that's all you should use it for. It's unethical and illegal to use customer data for purposes other than what was initially communicated. You must always act with a sense of responsibility.

Understanding the importance of ethics in AI reveals an exciting opportunity to lead with responsibility and innovation. Many businesses have already seen remarkable growth by leveraging AI effectively and ethically. In the following chapter, we'll explore these success stories to spark your inspiration. Ready for a dose of inspiration?

AI Accelerator

Here's a simple checklist to help you evaluate your current security measures in marketing.

Data Collection and Storage

- Are customer data collected only for necessary marketing purposes?
- Is data storage compliant with relevant privacy regulations (e.g., GDPR, CCPA)?
- Are encryption and secure protocols used for storing sensitive information?

- Are access controls in place to limit who can view and modify customer data?

Website Security

- Is the website secure socket layer (SSL)-encrypted (uses HTTPS)?
- Are regular security audits conducted to identify vulnerabilities?
- Are security plugins or software updated regularly?
- Is there protection against common threats like SQL injection, cross-site scripting (XSS), and cross-site request forgery (CSRF)?

Email Marketing Security

- Is email communication encrypted?
- Are measures in place to prevent phishing attacks (e.g., DMARC, SPF, DKIM)?
- Is the email list kept secure and not shared with unauthorized parties?
- Are unsubscribe and opt-out options easily accessible and functional?

Social Media Security

- Are strong, unique passwords used for social media accounts?
- Are multifactor authentication mechanisms enabled?

- Is employee access to social media accounts limited to those who need it?
- Are social media posts reviewed for potential security risks (e.g., revealing sensitive information)?

Third-Party Vendor Security

- Are third-party marketing tools and platforms vetted for security compliance?
- Are contracts with vendors clear about data handling and security responsibilities?
- Is there a process to regularly review and update vendor agreements?

Training and Awareness

- Are employees trained in security best practices relevant to marketing activities?
- Is there awareness training specifically tailored to phishing and social engineering attacks?
- Do employees know how to recognize and report security incidents related to marketing?

Compliance

- Is marketing activity compliant with relevant industry regulations and standards?
- Are there procedures in place to ensure compliance with laws such as CAN-SPAM and CASL?

- Are marketing campaigns reviewed to ensure they do not violate user privacy rights?

Incident Response

- Is there a documented incident response plan for security breaches related to marketing?
- Are roles and responsibilities clearly defined in the event of a security incident?
- Is there a process for communicating security incidents to affected parties?

Regular Audits and Reviews

- Are regular audits conducted to assess the effectiveness of security measures in marketing?
- Are security policies and procedures reviewed and updated regularly?
- Is feedback from security audits used to improve marketing security practices?

Backup and Recovery

- Are backups of marketing data regularly performed and securely stored?
- Is there a tested plan for recovering marketing data in the event of a breach or data loss?

By regularly reviewing and updating these aspects of security measures in marketing, you can better protect yourself and your customers from potential emerging threats in your business environment.

www.checkify.com/checklists/company-social-media-security-audit/

www.liveagent.com/checklists/marketing-audit-checklist/

INSPIRING BETTER USE OF AI ACROSS THE BOARD

The technology you use impresses no one. The experience you create with it is everything.

— SEAN GERETY

No matter how you feel about AI, there's no doubt that it's making waves in every industry. You know this, and you know your business needs it... and you also know that you need to get it right if it's going to be an asset to your organization. That's why you're here reading this... and it's why we at Matrix Press published this book.

We want to see AI being used wisely in every company we interact with... and we'd like you to keep this in mind as we ask you a small favor.

You can help encourage more business owners to make informed choices about integrating AI into their business practices, improving the experience of AI for all of us, no matter which side of the business-consumer relationship we're on.

Would you consider taking 5 minutes to leave your feedback online to help more business owners access these insights and approach their AI usage better informed?

By leaving a review of this book on Amazon, you'll show other business owners where they can find this information, which hopefully results in a better experience for everyone.

Reviews connect readers with the material they're looking for, so just a few words from you will make a difference.

Thank you so much for your support. AI is a great tool... but only when we use it well.

Scan the QR code below

CHAPTER 7: THE ART OF PERSONALIZATION
MARKETING SUCCESS STORIES

> *Commit to a niche; try to stop being everything to everyone.*
>
> — ANDREW DAVIS

According to Future Data Stats (2024), the use of AI in personalized marketing was worth more than $1.18 billion in 2023 globally, and this is expected to grow at a rate of 27% annually, with the market projected to be worth at least $77.5 billion in 2030.

AI has undeniably transformed the concept of personalized marketing, offering unprecedented insights, efficiency, and adaptability. As businesses continue to harness the power of AI, it promises even more engaging and relevant experiences for consumers. The fact that AI can analyze and process vast amounts of data in record time is not enough. For marketing purposes, this ability is useless if you cannot translate it into valuable customer-centric action. This is where personalization comes in, transforming the way you connect with your target audience.

One of the key strengths of AI lies in the fact that it can help you process and understand customer behavior at a deeper level. This is thanks to machine learning algorithms which help you identify user behavior patterns and trends. With this insight, you should be able to not only streamline the decision-making process but also reinvent your marketing strategies to meet individual consumer needs at a personal level.

Personalization has become an achievable reality in marketing thanks to AI. Smart algorithms analyze customer interactions, past purchases, and browsing history to deliver targeted content and recommendations. This not only enhances the customer experience but also significantly increases the likelihood of conversion.

Furthermore, AI makes it easier for you to adapt to changing consumer behavior in real time. As customer preferences evolve, your AI will continuously learn from their interactions with your business and adjust accordingly, ensuring that your marketing efforts remain relevant. This adaptability is a game-changer in an era where consumer expectations are constantly changing. It also makes your work efficient. By automating routine tasks, for example, email campaigns and social media posts, you free up HR and focus on more strategic aspects of marketing. This symbiotic relationship between AI and HR can empower your marketing team to tap into the depths of their creative skills while leveraging the power of AI for data-driven insights on the best way to meet your customers' needs.

Privacy concerns will always be there, and for that reason, you have to determine how to get the most value out of customer data in personalization without infringing on their individual rights to privacy.

In this section, we will explore some successful implementations of AI through the lenses of major corporations that a lot of people can relate to. The goal here is to show you that AI can turbocharge your marketing efforts. You might not have the kind of budget that these corporations have, but the AI field keeps evolving, and even on a tight budget, there'll always be something available to transform your marketing campaigns.

Your Needs Assessment

Imagine having a marketing strategy that appeals to the immediate needs of your audience and helps you preempt their preferences, and tastes according to what's trendy. That's the promise that AI brings to personalized marketing. This seems so good on paper. The question is how to make it happen.

First and foremost, you must understand and outline your current marketing landscape. What are your key objectives, pain points, and the areas you believe personalized marketing could make the most impact? The goal here is to figure out where your marketing efforts have been lacking, and what you can do to address that. At the same time, you're also trying to understand what your customers need and combine this knowledge to create an ideal compass to guide your marketing efforts.

The role of a needs assessment is to have a comprehensive roadmap that not only highlights your goals but also shows the practical steps you need to implement if you are to leverage AI effectively in personalized marketing. This is how you set the stage for a marketing strategy that not only speaks to your audience but does so in a way that makes them feel you are speaking directly to them. Here are some examples of how some of the biggest global brands managed to implement this strategy.

Coca-Cola

So, you know how billboards are usually the static giants on the roadside? Well, Coca-Cola decided to shake things up a bit.

Picture this: AI-powered billboards that don't just flash generic messages but instead, are tailored to the people passing by. It's like the billboards got an upgrade to mind-reading mode, but less creepy and way more awesome.

Coca-Cola tapped into the potential of AI to analyze real-time data—the time of day, the weather, the vibes in the air—you name it. Then, these smart billboards whipped up personalized messages and designs on the spot. Morning crowd? Boom, a refreshing "Good Morning" with a frosty Coke. Hot afternoon? How about a suggestion for an ice-cold Coke to beat the heat? It felt like Coca-Cola had a sixth sense of what people needed in that exact moment.

It didn't stop at billboards. Coca-Cola took the game to the next level by integrating this personalized touch into vending machines. Imagine walking up to a machine that doesn't just dispense your drink but also crafts a whole experience: your name on the screen and a cheerful greeting. Think of it like getting a virtual high-five from the vending machine, followed by your ice-cold soda.

The genius behind it all? AI algorithms doing their thing in real time, turning mundane billboards and vending machines into interactive moments. It wasn't just about selling a beverage; it was about creating a connection, a personalized, "Hey, we get you" vibe.

The results spoke for themselves. People weren't just walking by—they were engaging, sharing their experiences, and, of course, grabbing a Coke while they were at it. It was marketing that felt less like a pitch and more like a serendipitous encounter with a friend who knows exactly what you need. In a nutshell, Coca-Cola's foray into AI-powered personalization was more than your average marketing move—it was a masterclass in turning everyday moments into something extraordinary.

Starbucks

Let's turn our attention to how Starbucks took its personalized marketing game to the next level with a shot of AI. So, you know that feeling when you walk into a

Starbucks, and it seems like they've got your order down to an art? Well, there's some serious AI at play there.

Starbucks dove headfirst into the world of personalized marketing using AI algorithms as efficiently as some of the best baristas you've ever come across. The company started by analyzing your coffee journey—past orders, the time you usually swing by, and even the weather—once it became apparent that for a lot of people, coffee cravings tend to depend on the weather.

With this insight, it was able to create a personalized menu that pops up on your app, suggesting your go-to order or tempting you with a delightful twist based on your preferences. It's like having a virtual coffee sommelier whispering, "How about trying something new today?" Apart from that, you also have its AI suggesting some exciting offers in case you're in the mood to try something different.

Starbucks effectively managed to use AI to customize its marketing approach to individual preferences. Its customers didn't just feel understood, they could also satisfy their cravings while making some significant savings in the process. What Starbucks had managed to achieve was about more than selling coffee. It turned your typical coffee run into an experience that felt uniquely yours.

The best thing about it is that Starbucks was not going to use a one-size-fits-all approach. It fine-tuned its AI to recognize the diversity in tastes in its massive customer base. Therefore, it doesn't matter whether you're into the classic cappuccino or the latest trendy cold brew, its AI model can easily create a customized Starbucks experience for you.

The impact on revenue? Well, let's just say it wasn't your average caffeine boost. By serving up personalized recommendations and promotions, Starbucks kept customers coming back and enticed them to explore new flavors. This was a game-changer, because when it comes to beverages, many people tend to stick to the flavors they are used to, and hardly go about exploring. Yet, here was Starbucks, not only delivering a personalized experience but also enticing its customers to explore new blends.

Nike

Nike made a bold move into the world of personalized design by practically turning dreams into reality. It has always been a trailblazer in the industry, so turning to AI was a matter of when, not if. It didn't just stop at knowing your shoe size; it wanted to know more about user preferences and implemented an AI solution to analyze user activity within the Nike app, social media, and your previous shoe purchases.

With this information, it was able to build a personalized design for every user, inspired by your unique style, preferences, and insight into your social media activity. It's like having a design team dedicated to making shoes that scream "you." This is how Nike launched a series of limited-edition, shoe designs that were wearable expressions of individuality. From color palettes that matched user Instagram aesthetics to subtle nods to your favorite sports teams, each pair was a work of art designed to appeal to you at a personal level.

Before this, personalization was as simple as slapping your name on a shoe. Nike built on that with AI to create a brand that speaks to your soul. The buzz was real. Social media exploded with sneaker enthusiasts showing off their custom kicks, creating amazing hype. Instead of selling shoes, Nike was selling you a product that was uniquely yours, an experience.

In the end, its approach had evolved into something bigger than marketing. It intended to sell shoes that made a statement and left a lasting impression on the wearers and the people around them. Nike successfully highlighted how AI could transform personalization into an unstoppable force of creativity.

Agency Pure

Agency Pure simply spiced things up by harnessing the power of AI to understand its clients' audiences like never before. With access to data-driven insight, its AI could easily pinpoint what worked for its audiences, by analyzing metrics like their behavior, tastes, and preferences. Agency Pure started dishing out hyperpersonalized campaigns that felt like a one-on-one chat with each customer. Custom content, getting the right timing, and offers that practically said, "Hey, we've got exactly what you need."

All this was possible with the integration of rasa.io into their business model, which is how it was able to transform email marketing. Rasa.io is a platform that uses AI to personalize email newsletters. Its core functionality involves analyzing both the content of the newsletters and the behavior of the subscribers, helping businesses tailor the email content to individual preferences and increasing engagement by ensuring subscribers receive relevant and interesting content. With rasa.io, Agency Pure was able to dig deep into user preferences, analyzing what topics got its engines revving. That's how it was able to create newsletters that were more than informative, and eerily in sync with what each subscriber cared about.

With rasa.io, Agency Pure curated newsletters that made their audiences feel like they were handpicked just for them. By personalizing their marketing approach with AI, both Agency Pure and rasa.io turned revenue in a manner that would leave many chief financial officers green with envy.

Ultimately, what we can take from the examples above is that there's so much more to AI than most people realize. Integrating AI into your business model is not just about algorithms and data; it's about creating connections, marketing content that your audiences can relate to, and turning marketing into an experience that makes customers feel you went out of your way to think about them.

AI Accelerator

Here's a simple format to help you assess the success of AI in market personalization, and draw useful insight to supercharge your business going forward:

Business Background

- Considering what your business is about now, where do you want to take it?

_____

_____

- What challenges are you facing in your marketing efforts?

_____

_____

- Why should you choose AI for marketing personalization?

_____

_____

The AI Decision

- What is pushing you toward AI? Could it be your competitors, new trends, or something else?

  _____

  _____

- How do you choose the right AI tool or service?

  _____

  _____

AI Integration

- Come up with a step-by-step on how you intend to incorporate AI into your marketing.

  _____

  _____

- Outline the cost-saving methods you will use in this process

  _____

  _____

After Implementation

- Visible changes: Outline the significant benefits you observed from using AI

_____

_____

Feedback and Testimonials

- What do your customers say about the new personalized experience?

_____

_____

- How does your team feel about the enhanced capabilities?

_____

_____

The Roadblocks

- What challenges did you encounter after integrating AI into your personalization approach?

_____

_____

- How do you intend to overcome these challenges?

_____

_____

The Future of Your Marketing

- How do you plan to further use AI to enhance your marketing efforts?

_____

_____

Here are some more examples of how major brands have leveraged the power of AI to transform their businesses:

www.blog.socialmediastrategiessummit.com/10-examples-of-ai-in-marketing/

After seeing how AI revolutionized marketing for our case studies, you might be wondering about its role in recruitment. Get ready to dive into how AI is reshaping the way businesses hire employees in the next chapter!

PART THREE

AI POWERED RECRUITMENT SOLUTIONS

CHAPTER 8: TRANSFORMING HIRING WITH AI

> *You can dream, create, design, and build the most wonderful place in the world...but it requires people to make the dream a reality.*
>
> — WALT DISNEY

Did you know that an average hire requires a recruiter to spend 23 hours screening resumes and shortlisting applicants for interviews? (Naik, 2023) Now imagine if you can leverage AI to your advantage, and make this process seamless and cost-effective and spend less time on it, while still getting efficient results.

Integrating AI into hiring has proven to be a game-changer so far, for forward-thinking organizations. AI algorithms can go through resumes with lightning speed, filtering the perfect candidates based on their desirable skills, experience, and more importantly, if they are a cultural fit according to your desired metrics. This is one of the benefits of using AI in marketing, it works like a turbocharged assistant, freeing up valuable time for your recruitment team so they can focus on assessing the qualitative traits, which usually demand a human element at recruitment.

What's truly remarkable is the way AI brings a fresh perspective to the age-old problem of bias in hiring. By focusing solely on relevant qualifications, AI can help you create a level playing field for all applicants, promoting diversity and inclusion. Beyond recruitment, you can also tap into the power of predictive analytics to identify and nurture individuals who can be primed for future leadership positions. The thing about AI is that it allows you to not just find the right people for the job but also use its capacity to build a resilient workforce that will evolve and grow with your business.

Imagine a hiring process that streamlines candidate selection and provides invaluable insights for strategic decision-making. This is what you get with AI. From analyzing market trends like what other employers are looking for when recruiting for a certain position to predicting the possibility of success with each candidate in that position, AI transforms hiring into a data-driven, agile process. Instead of holding onto the power of task automation, you go a step higher and give your hiring team better insight into candidates, helping them make smarter decisions about who to bring on board.

This is how you build a workplace culture where talent thrives, and your business goals are met. More importantly, you build your business with a team that buys into your long-term vision. If you can implement AI into your hiring process, you should be able to build a resilient, diverse, and efficient workforce that can easily adapt to the evolving demands of the business market.

The Modern Recruitment Landscape and the Remote Revolution

One of the primary challenges in recruitment has always been that it is a time-consuming and manual process. Apart from going through countless resumes, you'll also have to conduct numerous interviews in person, and manage other logistical concerns, all of which can be an arduous task. The reliance on subjective assessments can sometimes lead to biases, affecting the selection of candidates.

With the advent of remote work, the geographical boundaries that once constrained talent acquisition are not as big a problem as they once were. Many employers are now tapping into a global pool of talent, necessitating a shift in recruitment strategies. Traditional methods struggle to adapt to this changing dynamic, often lacking the flexibility needed to identify and engage with candidates irrespective of their location.

Moreover, the ongoing digital transformation has revolutionized the skills required in the modern workplace. Many employers need candidates with expertise in emerging technologies, making it challenging for traditional recruitment approaches to keep up. The rapid evolution of skill sets and job roles requires a more agile and adaptive recruitment methodology.

Enter AI: the game-changer in the modern recruitment landscape. AI brings efficiency and objectivity to the hiring process. Automated screening of resumes, data insight into candidate matching, and predictive analytics that enable recruiters to identify top talent accurately. This not only reduces the time-to-hire but also minimizes the risk of biased selection. Besides, AI-powered tools can assess candidates based on a broader range of skills, going beyond the conventional qualifications recruiters usually look at. This is a significant advantage in a business world where hybrid roles and interdisciplinary skills are becoming the norm.

The modern employment space is dynamic and influenced by features like remote work, digital transformation, and the need for diversified skills. AI brings agility, efficiency, and objectivity, transforming your recruitment processes in a manner that puts you in a good position to get the most out of the talent pool at your disposal. Ultimately, the synergy between human intuition and AI will continue to redefine how businesses attract and retain talent in this new era of work.

Steps to Integrate AI Into Your Recruitment Process

Here's a simple guide to help you integrate AI into your recruitment process, streamline operations, and enhance decision-making.

Step 1: Assess Your Needs and Goals

Before diving into AI integration, evaluate your recruitment process. Identify pain points, bottlenecks, and areas where automation can bring efficiency. Set clear goals for the integration, such as reducing time-to-hire, improving candidate experience, or enhancing the quality of hires.

Knowledge of your organization's unique needs and setting clear goals is the foundational step in integrating AI into your recruitment process. This initial assessment helps identify specific issues and inefficiencies affecting your business, ensuring that the integration aligns with your overarching objectives, be it reducing hiring time, enhancing candidate quality, or improving overall efficiency.

Step 2: Define Key Metrics

Establish measurable KPIs to track the success of AI integration. These could include metrics like the time it takes to fill a position, candidate satisfaction, or the accuracy of candidate matches. This step is crucial for measuring the success and impact of AI integration. By establishing such quantifiable metrics, you create a framework for evaluating the effectiveness of AI tools. These metrics provide tangible insights into the areas where AI is making a positive contribution and areas that may require further optimization.

Step 3: Choose the Right AI Tools

Research and select AI tools that align with your goals and integrate seamlessly with your existing systems. Common AI applications in recruitment include resume screening, candidate matching, and chatbots for initial candidate interactions. Selecting appropriate AI tools is crucial in achieving successful integration. The right tools should align with your goals, seamlessly integrate with existing systems, and adhere to data protection regulations. Thorough research and careful consideration during the selection process ensure that the chosen tools effectively address the specific recruitment challenges your business is facing.

Step 4: Data Preparation and Integration

Clean and organize your existing data to ensure it's ready for AI analysis. Integrate AI tools with your applicant tracking system and other relevant platforms. The quality of data directly affects the accuracy of AI algorithms. Cleaning and organizing existing data sets prepares them for analysis, ensuring that the AI tools receive reliable input. Integration with applicant tracking systems and other platforms is essential for a seamless workflow, allowing AI to operate on up-to-date and relevant information.

Step 5: Employee Training

Provide training for your recruitment team on how to use and interpret AI insights. Address any concerns or misconceptions about AI, and emphasize that these tools are designed to support human decision-making, not replace it. Human–machine collaboration is at the core of successful AI integration. Comprehensive training for your recruitment team creates a deeper understanding of AI tools and their applications. This step not only equips your team with the necessary skills but also addresses any apprehensions, which is necessary to create a positive attitude toward AI as a valuable augmentation of human capabilities.

Step 6: Implement AI Gradually

Roll out AI integration in phases rather than all at once. Start with specific tasks or processes where AI can have an immediate impact, such as resume screening or initial candidate outreach. Introducing AI gradually allows for a smoother transition and minimizes potential disruptions. By starting with specific, well-defined tasks, you can gauge the impact of AI in a controlled manner. This phased approach enables your team to adapt gradually, fostering acceptance and understanding of the new tools.

Step 7: Monitor and Evaluate

Continuously monitor the performance of your AI tools and reassess their effectiveness over time. Regularly review KPIs and gather feedback from recruiters and candidates to identify areas for improvement and gather feedback for valuable insights into the strengths and weaknesses of the AI. Continuous monitoring and evaluation of AI performance are essential for ongoing improvement. This iterative process allows for adjustments, ensuring that the AI tools consistently meet your evolving recruitment needs.

Step 8: Ensure Ethical and Fair Practices

Pay attention to ethical considerations and potential biases in AI algorithms. Regularly audit and update the algorithms to ensure fairness and prevent unintentional discrimination. Ethical considerations in AI are paramount, especially in recruitment where biases can have significant consequences. Regular audits and updates to AI algorithms help maintain fairness and prevent unintended discrimination. Transparent communication with candidates about using AI fosters trust and ensures a fair and ethical recruitment process.

Step 9: Stay Informed and Adapt

It's always wise to stay informed about advancements in AI technology and recruitment trends. Adjust your AI strategy accordingly to remain competitive on the job market. Information on advancements and industry trends will be important in adapting your AI strategy over time. Regularly reassess your goals and adjust AI tools to ensure that your organization remains competitive and at the forefront of innovative recruitment practices.

Even as you follow the steps outlined, it's important to understand that the goal of this integration is not to replace your recruitment team but to enhance their work and expertise.

Choosing the Perfect AI Recruitment Solution

An ideal AI recruitment solution means more than just automating tasks. It should be about leveraging technology to enhance the entire hiring process. First, it should empower your recruiters by automating repetitive tasks like résumé screening, allowing them to focus on assessing candidates on qualitative skills and making strategic hiring decisions. The ideal solution should also integrate seamlessly with existing systems, providing a unified platform for managing candidate data and streamlining communication across teams. This ensures a smooth workflow and avoids the hassle of juggling multiple tools.

Besides, you should implement a solution that prioritizes fairness and diversity. By using algorithms that are transparent and free from bias, it helps ensure that every candidate is evaluated based on their skills and qualifications alone. Additionally, it should offer insights and analytics to help recruiters make data-driven decisions and continuously improve their hiring approaches. Ultimately, the ideal AI recruitment solution acts as a strategic partner, helping your recruiters attract top talent efficiently and effectively while upholding principles of fairness and diversity.

Let's break down the process of choosing the ideal AI recruitment solution to help you find something that suits your business needs.

Determine Your Unique Hiring Needs

First things first, know thyself. Dive deep into the quirks of your hiring process and figure out what you need to do differently. Identify what you need from an AI recruitment solution—whether it's speeding up the hiring process, improving candidate quality, or just making life easier for your team. Knowing your unique needs sets the stage for finding the perfect match. You could also find out what other employers in your industry are doing, and use that to assess the efficiency of your hiring process.

Project Evaluation

For any business solution, scalability is always an important consideration. You want a tool that can grow with your business, not struggle under pressure. Does it fit your budget? Usability is a deal-breaker; the best tool is worthless if your team can't use it seamlessly. How much will it cost you to train them on how to use it? And don't forget about support—you'll want a responsive lifeline if things get tricky.

The Need for Pilot Testing

Before you commit, pilot testing lets you see how the solution handles your unique hiring challenges, and ensures it's a perfect fit. This is how you catch any unexpected issues and make sure this AI tool is truly ideal for your business.

Reviews and Community Feedback

Dive into reviews and soak up the experiences of other business owners. What do they love about the tool? Where does it fall short? You're not alone in this journey, and learning from the collective wisdom of the business community can make a difference in how you approach this solution. This is an easy way to learn about the pros and possible cons that might not be so apparent in the company's write-ups.

Ultimately, finding the ideal AI recruitment solution is about compatibility, meeting your goals, and making sure you get a solution that works for you, just like your money.

AI Accelerator

AI Recruitment Mini Vision Board: Recruitment Challenges and Potential AI Solutions

The examples below show how to approach different problems in hiring and possible AI-driven solutions. Use them as a template to help you learn how to do the same for your business:

High Volume of Resumes

Challenge: Sorting through a large number of resumes can be time-consuming and overwhelming.

Potential AI Solution: Explore AI-powered resume parsing tools that efficiently analyze and categorize resumes, saving time and ensuring a more systematic screening process.

_____

_____

Diversity and Inclusion

Challenge: Struggling to achieve diversity goals and eliminate unconscious bias in the hiring process.

Potential AI Solution: Look into AI tools designed to mitigate bias in candidate selection, providing a fair and transparent evaluation process that enhances diversity and inclusion efforts.

___

___

Time-Consuming Screening Process

Challenge: Spending excessive time on initial candidate screenings can delay the overall hiring process.

Potential AI Solution: Consider AI-driven candidate screening platforms that automate the initial stages, allowing recruiters to focus on more nuanced aspects of candidate evaluation and engagement.

___

___

Inefficient Communication

Challenge: Coordinating communication between hiring teams and candidates can be fragmented and slow.

Potential AI Solution: Explore AI recruitment solutions with built-in communication features, facilitating seamless collaboration and timely updates among team members, recruiters, and candidates.

Lack of Data-Driven Insights

Challenge: Difficulty in tracking and analyzing key recruitment metrics for process improvement.

Potential AI Solution: Invest in AI platforms that offer robust analytics and reporting capabilities, enabling recruiters to gain valuable insights into metrics like time-to-hire, candidate quality, and other performance indicators.

Here are some useful resources that provide more insight into the role of AI in recruitment, which can give you more context on the discussion we've had so far:

www.linkedin.com/advice/1/how-do-you-identify-address-gaps-bottlenecks

www.resources.workable.com/tutorial/ai-for-recruitment

Having grasped the transformative power of AI in recruitment, it's crucial to address the elephant in the room: ethics and data security. Join us in the next chapter, where we demystify AI ethics and data security in recruitment.

CHAPTER 9: TRUST IN RECRUITMENT

AI ETHICS AND DATA SECURITY

> *There's nothing artificial about AI. It's inspired by people, it's created by people, and—most importantly—it impacts people. It is a powerful tool we are only just beginning to understand, and that is a profound responsibility.*
>
> — FEI-FEI LI

Ethical considerations act as the cornerstone for creating a fair and inclusive hiring process, one that ensures that AI algorithms do not inadvertently perpetuate biases or discriminate against certain demographics. By prioritizing ethical principles, you not only affirm your commitment to social responsibility but also cultivate a reputation for building a diverse and equitable workforce, something that many businesses have struggled to achieve over the years.

Looking at the immense volume of applicant data that you usually go through when vetting candidates, you'd definitely look into the prospect of using AI to streamline the process. Granted, AI is effective, but do you have the necessary security measures in place to assure all applicants that the integrity of the process will not be flawed?

The need for data integrity and confidentiality not only protects the privacy of job applicants but also shields your business from legal ramifications and reputational damage. Therefore, it's important to work toward a responsible balance between your desire for technological innovation and appropriate ethical considerations. How do you ensure the AI integration meant to handle the hiring process is done seamlessly, upholding human values and the integrity of your business?

Well, there are several things to consider, but first, let's assure applicants of their privacy because that's the only way you can be certain you're attracting the right personnel.

Ensuring Candidate Data Privacy

Employers are increasingly turning to technology to streamline their hiring processes, leveraging algorithms and machine learning to sift through lots of applications and identify potential candidates. While this approach offers efficiency and consistency, it also raises some challenges.

One notable advantage of automated decision-making in recruitment is the ability to analyze large datasets quickly. This is a good thing in that AI can help you identify desirable features in the applicants that you might not be able to easily notice in a short time on your own.

The beauty of this is that it allows your recruitment team to free up resources and focus on qualitative aspects of the hiring process. With this approach, you can be certain of a more objective hiring process, one that could even help you reduce employee turnover. It's all about not only getting the right people for the job but also making sure they share in your vision for your business.

That being said, you must still be careful in handling recruitment automation. A key aspect to manage effectively is the training data your AI system learns from. By proactively selecting and monitoring this data, you can mitigate risks and enhance the fairness and effectiveness of your recruitment efforts. This proactive approach not only improves the quality of your hires but also safeguards your business against potential pitfalls.

When all is said and done, transparency and accountability are essential features you should consider when implementing automated systems in recruitment. You need to clearly communicate how these systems work, ensuring that candidates understand the criteria used to evaluate their applications. Additionally, you should consider periodic audits to refine your algorithms so that they can identify and rectify any unintended biases that may emerge in the recruitment process over time.

The fact that you're automating this process doesn't mean that it's running on autopilot. You still need your HR team to pull their weight, albeit with better and more insightful data to work with. While automation can efficiently sift through resumes and initial qualifications, human judgment is essential for evaluating soft skills, whether the applicants are a cultural fit, and several other qualitative features in the candidate's resume.

An ethical hiring process, therefore, is the cornerstone of your business. This is how you bring in people who can buy into your vision and are committed to achieving your greater objectives.

While this implementation can be something you look forward to, it's also prudent to consider the possible challenges you might encounter in the process. Here's a brief overview of the benefits and risks you should be aware of.

Benefits

- **Efficiency boost:** Imagine a recruitment process that doesn't involve spending endless hours sifting through resumes manually. AI can streamline the initial screening process, allowing recruiters to focus on the cream of the crop. It's like having a personal assistant that never gets tired!
- **Objective decision-making:** AI doesn't have personal biases or bad days. It evaluates candidates based on predefined criteria, promoting fairness in the selection process. This can be a game-changer in creating diverse and inclusive teams.
- **Time-saving:** AI can analyze large datasets in a fraction of the time it would take a human. This

accelerates the hiring process and helps in identifying trends and patterns that might be overlooked by the human eye.

Risks

- **Algorithmic bias:** The Achilles' heel of AI in recruitment is the potential for bias. If the training data used to develop the AI models reflects some biases, it can perpetuate and even worsen existing inequalities. It's like trying to break free from bias but creating more systemic biases while at it.
- **Lack of human touch:** While AI is fantastic at crunching numbers, it might not always be the best tool, especially when you're trying to fill in positions that demand a human touch. AI cannot effectively assess a candidate based on their contextual understanding of situations, their emotional intelligence, and many other factors that are critical in the day-to-day running of your business. After all, there's no substitute for good old human intuition.
- **Privacy concerns:** AI relies on data, and lots of it. There's always a risk that the collection and analysis of personal information could encroach on applicant privacy. Given the ease with which people share personal information on social media, it's not easy to tow the fine line between respecting applicant privacy and identifying information that would make the hiring process more efficient.

- **Tech glitches:** Picture a situation where you're all set for a smooth interview process, and suddenly, your system breaks down. This is a possibility that could happen for different reasons. For example, power outages, network disruptions, server gremlins, and other technical issues that might not be solved immediately. What do you do then?

You can be certain that none of these challenges would disrupt an in-person interview. You'd probably sneak in a joke or two to make light of a tense moment, but the interview would still proceed on schedule.

It's clear that integrating AI into recruitment can at times be a double-edged sword. It brings unprecedented efficiency and objectivity to the table but requires careful handling to avoid some challenges that might disrupt the process or make it flawed.

Best Practices

Looking at the benefits and potential challenges above, you should implement some safeguards not only to protect candidate data but also to protect the integrity of your hiring process. If you don't already have one, develop a data protection policy so there are clear guidelines on protecting data and the people it represents. Begin by encrypting data both at rest and in transit. At rest, ensure that your databases, files, and backups are encrypted. In transit, use secure communication protocols (like HTTPS) to protect data as it passes through the digital ecosystem. Think of this like an invisibility cloak for your data.

The next step is to consider tokenization, a process where you replace actual data with tokens or random characters, making it practically impossible for unauthorized entities to decipher the true identity of the information. This way, even if someone manages to breach your defenses, all they get are virtual puzzles.

One thing you must remember is that not everyone needs the keys to the kingdom. Enforce strict access controls based on job roles and responsibilities. This minimizes the risk of internal snooping and ensures that only the right personnel can access certain levels of candidate data.

Build on that and adopt the principle of data minimization. Only collect and store the information you absolutely need for the recruitment process. The less you have, the less there is to protect. When it comes to user data, it's always advisable to use pseudonyms. These are aliases that are unlinkable without additional information. This adds an extra layer of protection, making it challenging for hackers to make sense of the encrypted data, even if they manage to get their hands on it.

I'd also encourage you to conduct routine audits of your security measures. Keep an eye on who accesses what and when. This helps detect any unauthorized attempts early on. As you work through this process, remember that tech exploits are always evolving. Stay updated on the latest encryption techniques. Regularly reassess your security to ensure it remains robust against emerging threats.

Transparent Data Handling Processes

When recruiting new members to your team, it's important to recognize that candidates invest not only their time but also their hopes and aspirations when applying for a position. When trust is nurtured, candidates feel valued and respected, fostering a positive candidate experience regardless of the outcome. Without trust, the recruitment process becomes a mere transaction, devoid of genuine connection and mutual understanding.

Maintaining trust in the recruitment process when utilizing AI is crucial to creating positive candidate experiences and ensuring fairness throughout the process. Here's how you can achieve this:

- **Candidate privacy and data protection:** Prioritize candidate privacy and adhere to data protection regulations. Clearly communicate how candidate data is collected, used, and stored throughout the recruitment process. Obtain explicit consent for data processing activities and ensure that candidates' personal information is handled securely and ethically.
- **Clear job descriptions:** When leveraging AI in recruitment, ensure that job descriptions are transparent and accurately reflect the role's responsibilities, requirements, and expectations. Ambiguity can lead to misunderstandings and erode trust between candidates and the hiring process.

- **Open communication:** Create open communication channels between candidates and the hiring team. Provide avenues for candidates to ask questions and receive timely responses throughout the recruitment process. Transparency builds trust and helps candidates feel valued.
- **Selection criteria:** Clearly define the selection criteria used to evaluate candidates. Whether it's skills assessments, cultural fit evaluations, or other criteria, transparency in the selection process ensures fairness and helps candidates understand how their candidacy is being evaluated.
- **Sharing feedback:** Offer constructive feedback to candidates, especially after interviews or assessments. This not only helps candidates understand areas for improvement but also demonstrates your commitment to their professional growth. Transparent feedback enhances trust and reflects positively on your business.
- **Transparency:** Be transparent about the role of AI in the recruitment process. Clearly communicate how AI tools are used, what data they analyze, and how they contribute to decision-making. Transparency mitigates concerns about bias and ensures candidates trust the integrity of the process.

Trust is important for the integrity and credibility of the recruitment process. Your reputation hinges on your ability to uphold fairness and transparency. When candidates trust that their qualifications and experiences are being fairly evaluated, it enhances the credibility of your business and the recruitment process as a whole. Conversely, any breach of trust can lead to reputational damage, dissuading top talent from engaging with your business in the future.

Training Data: The Origins of AI Bias

Training data plays an important role in the life cycle of AI. AI bias, in particular, often originates from the training data used to teach machine learning models. When data is collected, it inherently carries the biases and prejudices present in society. As a result, if the training data is skewed or lacks diversity, the AI model learns and replicates these biases in its decision-making process.

For instance, if historical hiring data is biased toward certain demographics due to past discriminatory practices, the AI model trained on this data may perpetuate those biases by favoring candidates from privileged groups while disadvantaging others. Here are some examples of bias that you might experience:

- **Bandwagon effect bias** arises when the predictions of a machine learning model are influenced by the popularity or prevalence of certain trends or beliefs, rather than objective data analysis. For instance, hiring teams might favor a certain technology skill simply because it is the current industry trend, not necessarily because it matches the company's needs.

- **Confirmation bias** occurs when the machine learning model selectively focuses on information that confirms existing beliefs or hypotheses, disregarding contradictory evidence. For instance, a recruiter might give more weight to positive information that confirms their initial impression of a candidate from a prestigious university, ignoring signs that the candidate may not fit the team well.
- **Exclusion bias** occurs when certain groups or data points are systematically excluded from the training dataset, resulting in incomplete or biased conclusions. For instance, screening processes that filter out candidates based on gaps in their employment history, missing potential top performers who took career breaks.
- **Observer bias** occurs when the individuals involved in collecting or analyzing data introduce their own subjective beliefs or preferences, influencing the results. Such as, an interviewer's personal preferences for certain hobbies or interests may influence their judgment, leading them to favor candidates who share similar interests.
- **Measurement bias** arises from inaccuracies or inconsistencies in data collection methods, distorting the outcomes of machine learning models. For instance, utilizing assessment tools that are not validated for the specific roles they are used to hire for, potentially misjudging a candidate's true capabilities.

- **Prejudicial bias** involves the inclusion of discriminatory or prejudiced views within the training data, leading to unfair treatment of certain groups. For example, cultural fit criteria that are too narrowly defined, favoring candidates who share similar backgrounds or lifestyles to current employees, potentially discriminating against those from diverse backgrounds.
- **Sampling bias** occurs when the training data isn't representative of the entire population, leading to skewed predictions. For example, using recruitment channels that only reach a certain demographic, such as job postings in industry-specific forums that not everyone accesses.

Being mindful of these biases is crucial in ensuring the integrity and fairness of your AI model. Moreover, your responsibility as a business owner is crucial in mitigating AI bias. By meticulously examining and preprocessing training data, you can identify and address biases before they become entrenched in the AI model.

Techniques such as data augmentation, sampling, and algorithmic fairness can help mitigate biases and promote more equitable outcomes. You could either task your IT team with this or discuss how to approach it with the team of developers behind the AI model you are using.

Mitigating AI Bias

How do you mitigate AI bias? You can think of this as a risk assessment approach because you're essentially trying to avoid a situation where you have an AI model that's efficiently running your business inefficiently.

First and foremost, you meticulously scrutinize the data inputs. Ensure that the datasets used for training are diverse and representative of the entire population, factoring in different demographics, cultures, and perspectives. This helps in reducing the chances of skewed results due to underrepresentation or misrepresentation of certain groups.

Additionally, you can implement preprocessing techniques to identify and mitigate biases within the data itself. This might involve techniques such as data augmentation, where you artificially increase the diversity of the dataset, or data anonymization to remove personally identifiable information that could lead to bias.

Another important step is to use fairness-aware algorithms during model development. These algorithms are designed to explicitly account for fairness metrics, such as demographic parity or equalized odds, to ensure that the AI system makes decisions without discriminating against any particular group.

I'd also encourage you to consider regular and thorough testing. This means continuously evaluating the AI system across different demographic groups to detect any biases that might have been overlooked during development. This iterative process helps in refining the model and making it more equitable.

Beyond testing, make a point of integrating transparency and accountability measures into the AI system. We've practically highlighted the importance of ethics and transparency in AI throughout this book, because this is what defines responsible AI and sets your business apart from others that harness the power of AI, albeit carelessly. This means that you should document the entire development process, including data collection, preprocessing, model architecture, and evaluation metrics, to ensure that all stakeholders understand how decisions are made and hold the system accountable for any biases.

AI Accelerator

Here's a simple checklist of potential biases you might encounter in your recruitment process. You can use this as a quick reference to help you create an ethical and fair recruitment process for your business.

Bias	Origin	Possible Solutions
Gender Bias	Traditional gender roles and stereotypes	Blind resume screening
	Unconscious biases of recruiters	Standardized interview questions
	Male-dominated industries or teams	Diverse interview panels
Racial Bias	Cultural stereotypes	Implementing structured interviews
	Historical discrimination	Using diverse sourcing channels
	Lack of diversity in your business	Providing unconscious bias training
Age Bias	Stereotypes about older or younger workers	Implementing age-blind recruitment processes
	Preference for younger candidates	Offering flexible work arrangements
	Fear of technology adaptation for older candidates	Ensuring diverse representation in hiring teams
Disability Bias	Misconceptions about disabilities	Providing accessible application processes
	Lack of understanding of accommodations	Offering reasonable accommodations during interviews
	Physical or digital barriers in the workplace	Educating staff on disability awareness
Socioeconomic Bias	Assumptions based on education or background	Ensuring job descriptions are inclusive and accessible
	Bias toward prestigious educational institutions	Providing opportunities for skills assessments
	Salary history requirements	Implementing fair and transparent salary policies

Further to the checklist above, here are some more resources to give you more context on how to evaluate your AI for bias:

www.equalai.org/assets/docs/EqualAI_Checklist_for_Identifying_Bias_in_AI.pdf

www.microsoft.com/en-us/research/project/ai-fairness-checklist/

Wrapping up this chapter, I encourage you to put yourself in the shoes of your candidates from time to time. You wouldn't want to engage in a recruitment process that is inherently disenfranchising, right? Now that you have the ideal setup for your business, with the right team, let's explore an important concept in business: sustainability. In the next chapter, we'll explore how to monitor and measure returns on your investment in AI.

PART FOUR
BUILDING AND SUSTAINING YOUR AI STRATEGY

CHAPTER 10: MONITORING, MEASUREMENT, AND ROI

> *Don't lower your expectations to meet your performance. Raise your level of performance to meet your expectations.*
>
> — RALPH MARSTON

The fact that AI is a game-changer is irrefutable. Most people have nothing but good words to say about AI's impact on their businesses. From streamlining customer service to improved cost efficiency, there's an endless list of benefits that your business can derive from AI. The question, however, is whether this is quantitative or qualitative.

Granted, every business owner hopes for qualitative gain. This is where the value lies. It's wholesome and defines the growth of your business as you conquer new heights. On the other hand, your AI approach was an investment. Like every other investment, you'd want to know whether it's been paying off or not, hence ROI. Sure, AI might have been great for your business, but how much of that is directly attributed to AI, and how much of that growth can you link to other factors, for example, a motivated workforce, refined product line, and so on?

The point here is that you can't just in totality, say that the growth you've experienced in your business is down to AI. Other factors could have contributed to it, and they too deserve credit. In this chapter, we try to put AI under the microscope, and help you figure out whether you're actually getting tangible value from AI, and if so, how much? With that, you can then walk back on your business processes and figure out what improvements can be made, whether they are AI-related or not, and how to get the most value from your AI. It's quite simple: Everyone must earn their keep, even AI.

As we edge closer to the end of this book, I want to highlight the immense value of measuring and monitoring the impact of AI on your business strategies. You must take an eagle-eye view to explore the broader implications of integrating AI in your business, and more importantly, whether the returns are tangible or otherwise. Since AI is the future, you can only stay ahead of the competition through innovation and a continuous commitment to maximizing cost efficiency.

The global AI market is expected to be worth more than $190 billion by the end of 2025 (Logan, 2019). Given what we've discussed in this book so far, how much of this market share do you intend to claim for your business?

Key Metrics to Gauge AI Success

Successful AI integration is about so much more than adopting cutting-edge technology; it's also about leveraging data-driven insights to push your business to greater heights. Three core metrics can help you figure out whether your integration has been a success or not: cost savings, customer engagement, and conversions. With these three under the microscope, it gets easier to pinpoint AI's role in improving your operational efficiency, customer satisfaction, and revenue growth. Let's explore these metrics in-depth.

Measuring Customer Engagement

Has your AI been useful in driving engagements on social media? Engagement is a key part of modern business, so this is one area where you'd really want to get as much insight as possible. Track the performance of AI algorithms in generating compelling content and creating meaningful interactions with customers online. Metrics such as likes, shares, and comments reflect the resonance of AI-driven content with your audience.

Next, you'll want to look at effectiveness in customer service, also known as customer satisfaction scores (CSAT). If you're using AI in customer service through chatbots or automated assistance, you'll need to regularly measure CSAT scores to gauge customer satisfaction. High CSAT scores indicate that AI is effectively resolving issues and leaving customers with a positive experience. CSAT is usually obtained through a survey asking customers to rate their satisfaction on a scale.

We also have the net promoter score, which gauges the loyalty of a business's customer relationships and their willingness to recommend a company's products or services to others.

Customer effort score measures the ease of interaction between a customer and your company. It can be obtained by asking customers to create the effort they had to put in to interact with your company.

Beyond that, you can also analyze metrics such as click-through rates on personalized emails, product recommendations, or targeted marketing campaigns. These are personalized points of engagement, so increased engagement with such content indicates the success of your AI in meeting customer expectations.

Maximizing Operational Efficiency

When it comes to operational efficiency, you'll probably be thinking about cost minimization. Note that costs, in this case, shouldn't just be limited to finances, and can also include other resources, for example, time. AI should not just enhance customer-facing processes as we've seen in the previous examples but also optimize internal workflows. Monitor your KPIs, for example, those related to time and resource utilization. This can be measured by tracking the time to complete tasks before and after implementation. Reduced time spent on routine tasks or streamlined workflows reflects the positive impact of AI on operational efficiency in your business.

How has your resource allocation changed since you implemented AI? Whether it's managing inventory or predicting customer demand, AI can minimize wastage and excess stock. Track different indicators and compare performance before and after you started using AI, to see whether AI contributes to tangible cost savings.

Operational Cost Reduction

AI allows you to automate routine tasks, minimizing the need for manual labor and reducing associated costs, especially in your marketing department. This not only enhances productivity but also mitigates the risk of human errors and helps to streamline your operations. As a result, you can easily redistribute your HR strategically, redirecting efforts towards more complex and value-driven activities, ultimately fostering a more efficient and cost-effective operational environment.

Furthermore, AI's ability to optimize resource allocation plays a crucial role in operational cost reduction. Machine learning algorithms can analyze vast datasets to identify patterns and trends, offering insights that empower you to make informed decisions around resource utilization in your marketing efforts. Whether it's predicting customer demand, optimizing inventory levels, or managing production schedules, the data-driven approach minimizes waste and maximizes operational efficiency. In essence, operational cost reduction as a metric encapsulates the transformative power of AI in fostering leaner, more resilient, and economically viable approaches to marketing.

Conversion Insights

The points above should culminate in revenue growth. The ultimate goal of AI integration is often increased conversions. Conversion rates simply measure the percentage of users who take a desired action. Analyze conversion rates before and after AI implementation. Assess whether AI-driven chatbots, personalized recommendations, or other strategies have positively impacted your conversion metrics.

At the end of the day, AI should help you get more value from your interaction with customers. This might also be a good point to try A/B testing to compare the performance of AI-driven strategies against traditional methods you've been using for a while. Whether it's website design, email campaigns, or product recommendations, A/B testing can provide valuable insights into the effectiveness of your AI.

Note that success with AI is not a destination but a continuous process. Reviewing the points we've discussed so far is not a one-time thing, but a continuous process to perform regularly to help you identify areas of weakness or how to refine your business strategy.

Evaluating ROI: Beyond Just Numbers

The value of AI to your business can either be tangible or intangible. As we mentioned earlier, it's always good to try and separate the direct and indirect influence of AI in your business to get a real picture of the actual value you're deriving from it. Here are some tangible, direct benefits you should be looking at:

- AI-driven tools can analyze customer behavior and preferences to offer personalized product recommendations, enhancing the chances of conversion. Chatbots and virtual assistants, for example, can provide real-time assistance, leading to improved customer satisfaction and increased sales.
- Think about your costs for a moment. Automating repetitive tasks can reduce labor costs, increasing operational efficiency in the process. If you're using predictive analytics tools, you can optimize anything from inventory management to stock management, thereby reducing costs.
- AI can help you streamline workflows, automate routine tasks, and help your employees in making faster and more informed decisions. This can directly boost productivity in your business.
- Another area where you'll appreciate AI is in marketing. AI can help you identify and target specific customer demographics, which makes it easier to improve the effectiveness of your marketing campaigns while at the same time reducing advertising costs.
- Finally, you can also look at tangible benefits in terms of customer service. Chatbots and virtual assistants can handle routine customer inquiries,

freeing up your team to handle escalated, complex issues. With more time to address pressing issues, you should see an improvement in customer satisfaction through better customer service.

Away from these direct benefits, let's shift our attention to intangible benefits. These might not be as apparent, but when you look at your business holistically, you'll realize the crucial role that AI has played in your growth.

- Adopting AI can enhance the perception of your small business as innovative and forward-thinking, contributing positively to your brand image. The fact that you're providing personalized and efficient services thanks to AI can create a positive customer experience, which is good for your brand reputation.
- Reputation comes with trust. Transparency in the use of AI can also build trust. If your customers understand how you're using AI to enhance their experience, they'll have an easier time trusting you. More importantly, being clear on data security and privacy can also help to build trust in your brand.
- AI-driven personalization creates a sense of being understood. This can create a deeper connection with your customers because they trust that you'll always find a way to take care of everything they need.
- AI could give you a competitive edge in the market by offering or pioneering innovative products,

services, or customer experiences that set you apart from your competitors.
- The more you use AI, the easier it gets to adapt quickly to changing market conditions by leveraging insights into dynamic trends and customer behavior. It's safe to say that AI can transform your decision-making process.

Success for your business, whether through AI or not, is a people-driven process. Even as you focus on your customers, don't lose sight of the people who matter the most—your employees. Automation, especially for mundane tasks, frees up their time, allowing them to focus on more creative and strategic aspects of their work. This is good for job satisfaction and overall morale. Note, however, that you can only achieve this when your people are a part of the process. Instead of imposing AI on them, make them a part of your strategy, so that they understand what you're working towards, and more importantly, their role in this transformation.

Continuously Refining Your AI Strategy

One important lesson we've pointed out throughout this book is the need to continuously evaluate and adjust your strategy. Nothing is cast in stone, especially not a business strategy. An effective strategy is flexible and can be adjusted as your needs change. What's the worst thing that could happen if you don't refine your strategy? As we mentioned earlier, there's nothing as bad as being so efficient at failure. AI can be so good, but at what? That's the risk you take if you don't tweak your strategy, a painful lesson that retail giant Amazon learned the hard way.

The case of Amazon's AI recruiting tool is a timely cautionary example of the potential pitfalls associated with biased training data and the unintended consequences of relying on AI in sensitive areas like hiring. Their ability to diagnose and correct a bias in their hiring data has become a helpful roadmap for other businesses. In this instance, the tool, which was designed to streamline the recruitment process, ended up perpetuating gender bias. This was purely because the algorithm was trained on predominantly male candidates' resumes. As a result, the AI was biased to prefer male candidates over female candidates (*The Guardian*, 2018).

This clearly shows you the critical importance of diverse and unbiased training data. AI algorithms are only as good as the data they are trained on, and if the training dataset lacks diversity or contains inherent biases, the algorithm may inadvertently reinforce and propagate the same. Your lesson, therefore, is to ensure that your training data is representative and free from discriminatory patterns to avoid unintended consequences, particularly in areas like hiring and decision-making. Remember, some of these decisions could have far-reaching legal and ethical consequences.

Amazon's case also underscores the need for continuous monitoring and ethical oversight not just in your AI solutions, but also for your strategy. After all, the solutions you implement are informed by your strategy. Scrutinize your AI solutions and implement safeguards to detect and mitigate biases. The goal here is to implement responsible AI. Don't forget that even though AI can provide amazing benefits, it requires careful handling and ethical considerations so you don't end up reinforcing or amplifying societal biases.

Lessons From Spotify's Recommendation AI

Spotify's success with its music recommendation AI is a testament to the power of leveraging AI to enhance user experiences and stay competitive. Their ability to analyze vast amounts of user data, for example, listening history and preferences, makes it easier to deliver highly personalized music recommendations. This level of data-driven personalization has significantly contributed to user satisfaction and retention, which explains why Spotify has quite a loyal user base, despite coming up against industry heavyweights who were established much earlier.

You can draw a critical lesson from this by recognizing the immense value of understanding and utilizing customer data effectively. Implementing AI solutions that can analyze and act upon customer behavior can help you create unique products, services, and marketing strategies tailored to meet the ever-evolving customer needs.

A key takeaway from this is the continuous learning aspect of Spotify's recommendation AI. By employing algorithms that adapt and improve over time, Spotify ensures its recommendations stay relevant as user preferences evolve. Your AI strategy, therefore, should embrace AI solutions that can learn from user interactions and adjust accordingly. This not only enhances the customer experience but also makes it easier to build a business that is responsive to changing market dynamics.

Finally, the integration of human touch alongside automation will be crucial in your AI strategy. While Spotify relies heavily on AI algorithms for music recommendations, it still relies on human curation for certain playlists. This hybrid approach strikes a balance, acknowledging that even though AI can analyze data efficiently, human intuition and creativity are still at the center of providing that personalized touch that keeps people coming back to their platform.

AI Accelerator

Your AI team can use the checklist below to evaluate progress on a regular basis, depending on the nature and volume of your business, and determine the effectiveness of your AI strategy.

Performance Evaluation

- Review and update KPIs for AI systems.
- Assess model accuracy and precision.
- Identify and document any significant deviations from expected performance.

Data Quality Check

- Verify the quality and relevance of input data.
- Address any issues related to data consistency and completeness.
- Explore opportunities to enhance dataset diversity.

Model Monitoring

- Implement or review monitoring systems for real-time model performance.
- Set up alerts for unusual behavior or deteriorating accuracy.
- Monitor model fairness and bias, if applicable.

Update Models

- Check for updated versions of pretrained models or algorithms.
- Evaluate the need for retraining models with new data.
- Ensure compliance with the latest industry standards.

Security Audit

- Conduct a security audit for potential vulnerabilities in AI systems.
- Review access controls and data encryption protocols.
- Address any identified security gaps promptly.

Regulatory Compliance

- Stay informed about changes in data protection and AI regulations.
- Ensure compliance with industry-specific standards (HIPAA, GDPR, and so on).
- Update privacy policies as needed.

User Feedback Analysis

- Gather feedback from end users regarding AI system performance.
- Analyze feedback for areas of improvement or emerging needs.
- Adjust models or algorithms based on user input.

Cost-Benefit Analysis

- Evaluate the cost-effectiveness of AI implementation.
- Consider opportunities for optimization and cost reduction.
- Assess the overall ROI of AI initiatives.

Collaboration and Training

- Organize collaboration between AI teams and other departments where applicable. (Hint: This is almost always applicable to keep a health organizational culture that embraces AI and the team.)

- Provide ongoing training for AI users.
- Stay updated on the latest advancements in AI technology.

Scalability Planning

- Assess the scalability of your existing AI infrastructure.
- Plan for increased data volumes and user loads.
- Consider hardware and software upgrades as necessary.

Documentation Update

- Update documentation for AI models, algorithms, and processes.
- Ensure that documentation is accessible to relevant stakeholders.
- Document any changes made during the month.

Social Responsibility Check

- Assess the overall impact of your AI applications on external stakeholders.
- Ensure ethical considerations are factored into AI decision-making.
- Review and update AI ethics guidelines.

CHAPTER 11: ADOPTING FUTURE AI DEVELOPMENTS

> *Some people call this artificial intelligence, but the reality is this technology will enhance us. So instead of artificial intelligence, I think we'll augment our intelligence.*
>
> — GINNI ROMETTY

We learn and get better with time. This, perhaps, is one of the greatest traits of humanity that we lent to AI. There's still a long way for AI to go, but it will certainly get better. As this happens, you must also figure out how to position your business for future growth, development, and the ultimate evolution of AI. Put strategies in place to build an AI-receptive culture that doesn't just adjust to the changing innovations around you, but also remains committed to your overall business goals, mission, and vision. More importantly, you must also create a culture of AI adaptability with the people you work with, because while AI can help you streamline your operation, the people help you achieve so much more at a personal level.

Running a business that easily adopts future developments in AI means always staying informed about the latest advancements and incorporating them into your business. This final chapter is the culmination of concepts we've discussed throughout this book. In a nutshell, here are some strategies that could help you stay on top of developments in different aspects of AI, and leverage them to grow your business:

- **Embrace continuous learning:** Stay updated on the latest research papers, publications, and news on AI. You can achieve this by following reputable resources, attending conferences, and participating in webinars, not only on AI but also about emerging technologies.
- **Networking and collaboration:** There's never been a better time to connect with professionals, researchers, and experts in the AI community. This is how you get valuable insights, access to resources, and opportunities for collaboration with like-minded persons, and grow your business in the process.
- **Experimentation:** Create a culture of experimenting within your business. Many people love to use tried and tested methods, but at times, it helps to go against the grain and try some outliers. As you explore new AI technologies, you'll understand their potential applications,

limitations, and how adaptable they are in your business.
- **Skills development:** We've already established the fact that AI gets better over time. Likewise, invest in training programs for your team so you are surrounded by people with the right skills, and capable of using the latest AI technologies and tools to nurture and grow your business.

The most important thing if you're building your business for adaptability is to be proactive. You're building or running a business in a generation that has witnessed some of the finest innovations in human history yet. Change is imminent, so you must embrace a mindset of continuous improvement to effectively position your business to adapt and benefit from future developments in AI.

Ensuring Your AI Solutions Stay Relevant

Would you believe me if I told you that Kodak developed the world's first digital camera? Yet, the company faded into oblivion.

Kodak was once a mainstay in the film photography industry, a household name for decades. In a world where photography is appreciated more than ever, it's a pity that Kodak couldn't adapt not just to the technological advancements, but the dynamic customer needs. When everyone was embracing the digital dimension, Kodak stayed true to its traditional film-based model. Unfortunately, heritage couldn't carry it through this.

Beyond heritage, here are some other reasons why Kodak failed:

- It struggled to shift from film to digital photography as the world evolved. It ended up holding onto its traditional film-based business model longer than it should have.
- Kodak failed to effectively capitalize on its early digital imaging innovations, including the fact that it built one of the first digital cameras in 1975.
- Despite holding valuable patents, Kodak couldn't successfully monetize them compared to more successful competitors.
- The company's corporate culture and leadership limited its ability to embrace new technologies.
- Ultimately, it was only a matter of time before declining film sales and unsuccessful digital initiatives plunged Kodak into financial challenges, leading to its bankruptcy in 2012.

Unfortunately, while Kodak struggled, its competitors improved, eating into its market position and winning over most of its loyal customers. The lesson you can take from this is the value of adaptability. Everything around you evolves. With AI, this evolution in the business environment happens much faster than before, so you must adapt.

The rapid pace of AI growth poses solutions and problems for your business in equal measure: solutions if you can adapt, but problems if you're too slow and fall behind. By integrating AI into your business model, you're looking at lower operating costs, improved productivity, and greater innovation, among other benefits. If you don't adapt promptly, your competitors get ahead, and going by the example of Kodak, there may be no coming back from that.

Here are some useful tips to help you stay updated on the latest developments in AI:

- Several reputable media outlets publish news on developments in AI, for example, AI News, The AI Report, and Synced. You can also read AI research journals, for example, the *Nature Machine Intelligence* and *Journal of Artificial Intelligence (JAIR)*. Note that even the fact that these outlets are relevant today doesn't mean that they'll remain relevant in perpetuity.
- You could also join AI communities and interact with luminaries, enthusiasts, researchers, and other people on developments in AI.
- Be on the lookout for major AI conferences, for example, Conference on Neural Information Processing Systems, International Conference on Machine Learning, and Association for the Advancement of Artificial Intelligence. These conferences often publish cutting-edge research. Follow their official social media accounts and their websites for updates.
- Subscribe to newsletters from organizations, research labs, and companies that are leading the charge on AI, for example, OpenAI, Google AI, and Meta Platforms (formerly Facebook Inc.).

- Follow renowned AI researchers on their social media platforms, for their thoughts on the latest developments in the sector, or updates on what they are working on.
- Enroll in online courses or attend webinars offered by universities and organizations to gain insights into the latest advancements in AI.

While the strategies above can help you make significant strides in integrating AI into your business, the most effective approach is implementation. Hands-on experience will always give you the most practical solutions for your business. Try different AI tools and frameworks, coding exercises, and AI projects. This will give you a deeper understanding of what works for you and what doesn't.

The knowledge you gain from the sources we've discussed above will only be useful when put into practice. With that, you can review and update your AI strategies and keep your business thriving in a highly competitive business world. Here are some questions you need to think about that can transform your AI strategy going forward.

What's the nature of your content?

Think about the kind of content that drives your business. Is it still relevant? Do you need to improve it or change it altogether? How's your audience engaging with your current content? With AI, you can get more insight into audience sentiment, identify gaps in your audience funnel, analyze keywords, hashtags, and trends, and improve content performance.

How can you improve your content?

This comes down to engagement with your audience. Once you understand the nature of your content as outlined above, the next step is to analyze the best-performing content to find how you can either expand its performance across the board or enhance it.

How consistent is your brand?

Consistency is key to quality brand engagement. You can use AI tools like writing assistants to figure out the style and tone of your content. It could be anything from your social media posts to email newsletters. Does your tone still appeal to your audience as it once did?

The final step in making sure your AI solutions are relevant is to consider applicable legislation or regulations. This is a vastly evolving field, so it's important to review and update your policies regularly. The last thing you want to do is to be using outdated solutions. Always keep an eye on industry requirements or best practices, legislation, and policy.

Building a Culture of AI-Driven Innovation and Adaptability

Don't be skeptical about AI. Embrace it like Outpace Coaching did. Its approach to an AI-driven business was to develop Pacey, an AI coach. They had product experts train Pacey on how to help their customers succeed, and ultimately, Outpace Coaching's customers' success translated to the overall success of the business.

This is proof that small businesses can thrive by adapting to the AI and innovation-driven demands of business. Most people believe that only big businesses can tap into AI's infinite potential, but small businesses like Outpace Coaching continue to disapprove this flawed ideology.

The Need for a Change-Oriented Business Culture

Adaptability will be crucial in maintaining or growing your position in the market in the face of stiff competition. To achieve this, some of the words that you can use to describe your business include resilient, innovative, and agile. These are also prerequisites for an enabling environment that spurs business growth.

Now, let's think beyond the business a bit. How do your employees fit into this culture of change? Your role as an entrepreneur is to create a conducive environment for your team to thrive. With such a culture in place, you create room for your creative thinking, flexibility, and a workforce that can easily embrace new ideas. This is the healthy work environment that champions the kind of innovation that drives your business forward with positive results. A change-oriented culture in a healthy business environment is key to greater employee retention and satisfaction.

Instilling a change-oriented culture is a team effort. Here are some simple strategies that you can implement together with your employees. Remember, you have a higher chance of success if your team rallies behind your AI agenda, hence the need for collaborative effort.

Continuous Learning

This is important to ensure that leadership and management understand the potential impact of AI on the organization. Involve your team in developing a clear vision for how AI aligns with business goals and strategy. To guide the continuous learning initiative, establish a roadmap for AI integration, and communicate it to the entire organization.

Raise Awareness

Conduct awareness sessions to educate employees about AI and its implications on their roles and the organization. Use these sessions to address any misconceptions or fears they might have, emphasizing the fact that you're using AI as a tool to enhance their capabilities rather than replace them.

Strategic Implementation

Identify specific use cases where AI can add value to your business operations. Your employees' input will be quite valuable in this, so involve them in the identification process to gather insights into their workflows, pain points, and more importantly, their suggestions on where and how AI can improve their processes.

Skills Assessment

Assess the current skill sets of your team to identify gaps you could improve with AI. Building on that, come up with training programs to upskill employees in areas where they might have fallen short. For example, you could explore lessons in data literacy, programming, and knowledge of AI algorithms.

Note that these training sessions can only be effective when they are targeted, instead of a scattergun approach. Training takes time, money, and other resources, so invest in value-adding material through workshops, specific courses, or even strategic partnerships with relevant learning institutions.

Change Management

While change might be good for your business, there's no guarantee that it will be easy. Implement effective change management strategies to help employees adapt to the new work structures. Build ongoing support and resources into your business processes to manage the psychological aspects of change. To this end, establish feedback loops to gather insights from your team about the impact of AI on their roles and workflows. This feedback will be useful in continuous improvements to your AI strategy and training sessions for your team.

As you work toward a culture of change in the business, go the extra mile and foster a learning culture. We learn throughout our lifetime. This means creating room for errors and mistakes and growing from them.

The strategies above will help you achieve more than a change-driven approach to running your business. You'll have effectively created an informed and supportive business environment that fosters growth for both your business and the people working for or with you.

AI Accelerator

Monthly AI Trends Journal

Note: You can update this daily, weekly, or at whatever frequency that fits your business strategy. The template below is for a weekly strategy.

Date: _____

AI Trend Learned:

_____

_____

_____

Brief Description:

_____

_____

Potential Applications for Our Business:

_____

_____

Considered Implementation Strategies:

_____

_____

Challenges and Adjustments Identified:

_____

_____

Next Steps:

_____

_____

Reflections at the End of the Month

Key Themes Identified:

_____

_____

Patterns or Connections Observed:

_____

_____

Notable Success Stories or Case Studies:

_____

_____

Areas for Further Exploration:

_____

_____

Action Plan for Next Month:

_____

_____

Here's an example using the template above:

AI Trend Learned: NLP advancements.

Brief Description: NLP has seen significant improvements, particularly in sentiment analysis and language translation.

Potential Applications for Our Business: Implement NLP in customer support chatbots to enhance understanding and responsiveness and improve response times.

Considered Implementation Strategies: Pilot a chatbot with NLP capabilities for a specific product or service, and measure customer satisfaction and response times.

Challenges and Adjustments Identified: Potential language nuances and accuracy concerns. Consider ongoing training and updates for the NLP model.

Next Steps: Schedule a meeting with the IT and customer support teams to discuss a pilot program.

Reflections at the End of the Month:

- Identified a common theme of improving customer experience through AI technologies.
- Noticed the need for interdisciplinary collaboration between IT, customer support, data science, compliance, logistics, and inventory management.

Action Plan for Next Month:

- Targeted investigation into the applications of generative adversarial networks in creative content generation.
- Participation in an AI ethics and governance webinar for all relevant teams.
- Initiate a company-wide training program on the basics of AI and its potential impact on various departments.

PLEASE REVIEW
LEAD THE AI REVOLUTION!

AI is going to come on in leaps and bounds over the coming years, and now that you're on board, your business will grow with it. This is the time to lead other businesses toward the revolution!

Simply by sharing your honest opinion of this book and a little about your own experience with AI, you'll inspire other business owners to explore its potential for their organizations.

We Want Your Feedback!

Thank you so much for your support!

Scan the QR code to leave a review.

CONCLUSION

The journey into implementing S.M.A.R.T. AI in business can be nothing short of transformative; And the fusion of S.M.A.R.T. criteria with AI technology offers an unparalleled opportunity to enhance efficiency, productivity, and strategic decision-making within your business.

We've witnessed the power of specificity in guiding AI initiatives towards well-defined goals. The emphasis on measurability provided a metric lens to evaluate success and fostered a culture of continuous improvement. Achievability, a cornerstone of the S.M.A.R.T. framework, also acted as a guiding light, one that ensures your AI endeavors are practical. One thing that's been evident throughout our discussion is the relevance of AI in different business environments.

AI is adaptable by design, so if you're to make it work for you, you have to work it around your business in a scalable manner. This is why we stressed the importance of needs assessment and aligning your goals, vision, and objectives in every AI implementation in your business.

We covered some real-world examples and case studies that prove that S.M.A.R.T. AI is not merely a theoretical framework but also a tangible catalyst that can transform your business. The success stories of businesses leveraging the power of AI like Coca-Cola and Nike underscore the profound impact it can have on operational processes, customer engagement, and your bottom-line results. From streamlining supply chains to personalizing customer experiences, the applications are boundless, promising a future where businesses can thrive on the cutting edge of technology.

However, it is crucial to acknowledge the challenges and ethical considerations that accompany the integration of AI into your business practices. The responsible development and deployment of AI technologies require a commitment to transparency, fairness, and ongoing evaluation of its potential impact on your business model. Thus, you must strike the right balance between innovation and ethical considerations to shape the future landscape of AI in your business. Remember that once you implement AI, it becomes an ongoing process, one that requires continuous evaluation and adjustment.

When it comes to AI, you must also pay attention to the intricacies of implementation strategies, data governance, and the collaborative efforts required to bridge the gap between human intuition and machine intelligence. The only way AI can work for you is if you cultivate a mindset of continuous learning and adaptability. Implementing AI in your business is not a static destination but a dynamic journey, one that requires you to stay agile and responsive to evolving technologies and market dynamics.

For modern businesses, the role of AI is the cornerstone upon which innovation and efficiency are built. From optimizing internal processes to enhancing customer experiences, the integration of AI technologies sets the stage for a transformative landscape for your business that is not only forward-thinking but can also dynamically respond to evolving market demands. It's safe to say that AI will help you stay ahead of the pack if you use it well.

Effective chatbot strategies, for example, represent an important phenomenon in the business world today, where the convergence of AI and customer interaction takes center stage. Chatbots are not merely automated responses but sophisticated tools that can significantly elevate customer engagement. With the right chatbot tools, you'll be able to meet specific business goals and adapt and learn more over time from customer interactions, becoming invaluable assets in fostering meaningful connections with your clients.

In an era where data is king, the responsible use of AI technologies is paramount. Your implementation must take into account concerns related to data privacy, algorithmic bias, and the imperative need for robust security measures. Balancing innovation with ethical considerations should always be the guiding principle for your business, not just for AI, but any other technological intervention you integrate into the business.

We considered the use of AI in personalizing marketing strategies, a concept that has been perfected by some of the biggest brands in the business world today. It's all about harnessing the power of data and AI to create tailored concepts with a personal appeal to your customers. Looking at the success of the businesses using this concept, it's clear that if you can tap into the power of AI for personalization, you have a better chance at forging stronger connections with your target audience, and ultimately driving brand loyalty and growing your market share.

AI's footprint in the business landscape will continue to expand, growing in both reach and potency. As we draw to the end of this journey into the realm of S.M.A.R.T. AI for businesses, it's crucial to remember that the landscape of technology is ever-evolving. The tools, strategies, and insights shared in this guide aim to provide a solid foundation, but the real magic lies in continuous learning and adaptation.

AI will get better with time, and with some focused effort, your business can harness its transformative power. The AI path is paved with greater efficiency and profit, and the business world is on the brink of the greatest industrial revolution in its history! Your business, large or small, can be a part of it. Welcome to the techno-magic that is the age of AI!

It's still magic even if you know how it's done.

— TERRY PRATCHETT.

REFERENCES

Abbamonte, K. (2023, April 13). *AI job search tips: 9 AI tools to help you land your next job.* Zapier. https://zapier.com/blog/ai-job-search/

Accenture. (2017). *Accenture report: Artificial intelligence has potential to increase corporate profitability in 16 industries by an average of 38 percent by 2035.* https://newsroom.accenture.com/news/2017/accenture-report-artificial-intelligence-has-potential-to-increase-corporate-profitability-in-16-industries-by-an-average-of-38-percent-by-2035

Agouridis, A. (2023, February 9). *AI in recruitment - Everything you need to know.* Jobylon AB. https://www.jobylon.com/blog/how-ai-is-transforming-the-world-of-recruitment

Aha! (2021). *What is technology gap analysis?* https://www.aha.io/roadmapping/guide/it-strategy/technology-gap-analysis

Ahmad, M. H. (2022, June 16). *Hyper-personalized marketing: What's in stake, what matters the most?* LinkedIn. https://www.linkedin.com/pulse/hyper-personalized-marketing-whats-stake-what-matters-ahmad/

AIContentfy Team. (2023a, March 5). *The role of AI in content personalization.* AIContentfy. https://aicontentfy.com/en/blog/role-of-ai-in-content-personalization

AIContentfy Team. (2023b, May 30). *The ethics of AI marketing: Balancing personalization and privacy.* AIContentfy. https://aicontentfy.com/en/blog/ethics-of-ai-marketing-balancing-personalization-and-privacy

AIContentfy Team. (2023c, November 6). *The role of AI in content customization.* AIContentfy. https://aicontentfy.com/en/blog/role-of-ai-in-content-customization

AIContentfy Team. (2023d, November 7). *AI tools vs human insight: Striking a balance in marketing.* https://aicontentfy.com/en/blog/ai-tools-vs-human-insight-striking-balance-in-marketing

Aizenstros, J. (2020, December 11). *Ethical sourcing of consumer data: Obstacles and considerations.* Retail TouchPoints. https://www.retailtouchpoints.com/features/executive-viewpoints/ethical-sourcing-of-consumer-data-obstacles-and-considerations

Al-Katib, A. (2020, June 18). *How to avoid stereotypical biases in AI.* Mission

Critical Magazine. https://www.missioncriticalmagazine.com/articles/93049-how-to-avoid-stereotypical-biases-in-ai

Anand, A. (2023, February 27). *Anonymization, de-anonymization and encryption for machine learning*. LinkedIn. https://www.linkedin.com/pulse/anonymization-de-anonymization-encryption-machine-learning-anand/

Andrades, G. (2023, July 12). *The evolving landscape - AI's impact on gap analysis in testing*. ACCELQ. https://www.accelq.com/blog/gap-analysis-in-testing/

Appen. (2022, March 3). *How artificial intelligence data reduces overhead costs for organizations*. https://www.appen.com/blog/how-artificial-intelligence-data-reduces-overhead-costs-for-organizations

Barney, N. (2023). *6 ways to reduce different types of bias in machine learning*. TechTarget. https://www.techtarget.com/searchenterpriseai/feature/6-ways-to-reduce-different-types-of-bias-in-machine-learning

Becher, J. (2014, July 7). *SAP BrandVoice: Douglas Adams' technology rules*. Forbes. https://www.forbes.com/sites/sap/2014/07/07/douglas-adams-technology-rules/?sh=6a6a2a6753e6

Bigelow, S. J., Pratt, M. K., & Tucci, L. (2023). *SWOT analysis (strengths, weaknesses, opportunities and threats analysis)*. TechTarget CIO. https://www.techtarget.com/searchcio/definition/SWOT-analysis-strengths-weaknesses-opportunities-and-threats-analysis

Blehar, M. (2023, September 28). *6 examples of companies successfully using an AI recruiting platform*. Phenom. https://www.phenom.com/blog/examples-companies-using-ai-recruiting-platform

BotPenguin. (2023, June 22). *Feedback chatbot*. https://botpenguin.com/glossary/feedback-chatbot

Burt, A. (2023, May 16). *The digital world is changing rapidly. Your cybersecurity needs to keep up*. Harvard Business Review. https://hbr.org/2023/05/the-digital-world-is-changing-rapidly-your-cybersecurity-needs-to-keep-up

Buxy, S. (2022, July 8). *Why conversational AI is becoming essential for customer service*. Conversation Design Institute. https://www.conversationdesigninstitute.com/blog/why-conversational-ai-is-essential-for-customer-service

Calciano, D. (2023, February 22). *AI in the workplace: The future of business efficiency and cost savings*. LinkedIn. https://www.linkedin.com/pulse/ai-workplace-future-business-efficiency-cost-savings-daniel-calciano/

Candelon, F., Chu, M., Jha, G., Khodabandeh, S., Kiron, D., & Schrage, M.

(2023, August 4). *How A.I. can transform your company's performance—and measure it better*. Fortune. https://fortune.com/2023/08/04/ai-performance-metrics-kpis/

Casey, K. (2021). *How to get your resume past artificial intelligence (AI) screening tools: 5 tips*. The Enterprisers Project. https://enterprisersproject.com/article/2021/3/artificial-intelligence-ai-screening-tools-how-build-resume-5-tips

CBS News. (2023, March 6). *ChatGPT and large language model bias*. https://www.cbsnews.com/news/chatgpt-large-language-model-bias-60-minutes-2023-03-05/

Charest, D. (2023, October 3). *AI stats and trends for small business marketing*. CPA Practice Advisor. https://www.cpapracticeadvisor.com/2023/10/03/ai-stats-and-trends-for-small-business-marketing/95053/

Checkify. (2019, July 4). *Social media security audit checklist*. https://checkify.com/checklists/company-social-media-security-audit/

Chen, X., Xie, H., Zou, D., & Hwang, G.-J. (2020). Application and theory gaps during the rise of Artificial Intelligence in Education. *Computers & Education: Artificial Intelligence, 1*, 100002–100002. https://doi.org/10.1016/j.caeai.2020.100002

Chen, Y., Prentice, C., Weaven, S., & Hisao, A. (2022). The influence of customer trust and artificial intelligence on customer engagement and loyalty – The case of the home-sharing industry. *Frontiers in Psychology, 13*. https://doi.org/10.3389/fpsyg.2022.912339

Cherniak, K. (2023, October 19). *Chatbot statistics: What businesses need to know about digital assistants*. Master of Code Global. https://masterofcode.com/blog/chatbot-statistics

Church, B. (2023, September 5). *5 types of chatbot and how to choose the right one for your business*. IBM. https://www.ibm.com/blog/chatbot-types/

Coca-Cola Company. (2023a, March 20). *Coca-Cola invites digital artists to "create real magic" using new AI platform*. https://www.coca-colacompany.com/media-center/coca-cola-invites-digital-artists-to-create-real-magic-using-new-ai-platform

Coca-Cola Company. (2023b, September 12). *Coca-Cola® Creations imagines year 3000 with new futuristic flavor and AI-powered experience*. https://www.coca-colacompany.com/media-center/coca-cola-creations-imagines-year-3000-futuristic-flavor-ai-powered-experience

Codecademy. (2018). *Ethics of chatbots*. https://www.codecademy.com/article/ethics-of-chatbots

Cohen, B. (2022, June 15). *How Spotify uses AI to create an ultra-personalized customer experience and what distributors can learn from it*. Distribution Strategy Group. https://distributionstrategy.com/how-spotify-uses-ai-to-create-an-ultra-personalized-customer-experience-and-what-distributors-can-learn-from-it/

Collibra. (2024). *AI readiness checklist*. https://www.collibra.com/us/en/resources/ai-readiness-checklist

Coniq. (2023, February 6). *How to personalize the customer experience*. https://www.coniq.com/resources/personalize-the-customer-experience/

Consolante, M. (2019). *Using dynamic content to deliver personalized experiences*. Acquia. https://www.acquia.com/blog/how-marketers-use-dynamic-content-deliver-personalized-experiences

Correlation One. (2023, June 23). *5 barriers to AI readiness and how to overcome them*. https://www.correlation-one.com/blog/5-barriers-to-ai-readiness

Cote, C. (2021, March 16). *5 principles of data ethics for business*. Business Insights Blog. https://online.hbs.edu/blog/post/data-ethics

Das, A. (2023, July 19). *How artificial intelligence is transforming the learning technology landscape*. eLearning Industry. https://elearningindustry.com/how-artificial-intelligence-is-transforming-the-learning-technology-landscape

The Data Scientist. (2023, June 7). *The role of AI in modern marketing: Enhancing efficiency and effectiveness*. https://thedatascientist.com/the-role-of-ai-in-modern-marketing-enhancing-efficiency-and-effectiveness/

Davenport, T. H., Grewal, D., & Guha, A. (2021). *How to design an AI marketing strategy*. Harvard Business Review. https://hbr.org/2021/07/how-to-design-an-ai-marketing-strategy

Davis, A [@DrewDavisHere]. (2014, June 11). *"Commit to a niche; try to stop being everything to everyone." Andrew Davis http://sumo.ly/MBa thanks @Profoundryco* [Post]. X. https://twitter.com/DrewDavisHere/status/476675613772619776

DeGance, J. (2023, April 27). *AI-driven marketing strategies for the future era of customer engagement*. LinkedIn. https://www.linkedin.com/pulse/ai-driven-marketing-strategies-future-era-customer-jocelyn-degance/

Delesline, N., III. (2022, August 31). *Here's how one tech company uses data to enhance recruitment and hiring diversity*. ZDNET. https://www.zdnet.com/education/business-management/tray-io-data-driven-recruitment/

Devane, H. (2022a, May 13). *What are the top data anonymization techniques?*

Immuta. https://www.immuta.com/blog/data-anonymization-techniques/

Devane, H. (2022b, May 18). *The top 5 data anonymization best practices.* Immuta. https://www.immuta.com/blog/data-anonymization-best-practices/

Dilmegani, C. (2024). *Top 14 chatbot best practices that increase your ROI in 2024.* AIMultiple. https://research.aimultiple.com/chatbot-best-practices/

Dilmegani, C. (2024). *Why does AI fail?: 4 reasons for AI project failure in 2024.* AIMultiple. https://research.aimultiple.com/ai-fail/

Disney, W. (n.d.). *Walt Disney quote.* BrainyQuote. https://www.brainyquote.com/quotes/walt_disney_131631

Doan, D. (2024, February 23). *7 marketing questions teams are asking in 2024 (+Data & Insights).* HubSpot. https://blog.hubspot.com/marketing/marketing-questions

Dorfer, T. A. (2023, January 7). *How to stay on top of the latest AI research.* Towards Data Science. https://towardsdatascience.com/how-to-stay-on-top-of-the-latest-ai-research-e8993523ef3e

Dowd, E. (2021, September 28). *3 case studies of SMBs using AI for marketing.* Marketing AI Institute. https://www.marketingaiinstitute.com/blog/3-case-studies-of-smbs-using-ai-for-marketing

DX Adobe. (2024). *What is predictive modeling in marketing?* Adobe Experience Cloud Blog. https://business.adobe.com/blog/basics/predictive-modeling

Einstein, A. (n.d.). *Albert Einstein quote.* BrainyQuote. https://www.brainyquote.com/quotes/albert_einstein_164554

Etzioni, O. (n.d.). *Oren Etzioni quote.* BrainyQuote. https://www.brainyquote.com/quotes/oren_etzioni_931691

Existential Risk Observatory. (2023, November 30). *Unaligned AI.* https://www.existentialriskobservatory.org/unaligned-ai/

Fahmi, A., Cariappa, A., & Guney, G. (2014). *Real time marketing analytics: Customer data optimization best practices.* TTEC. https://www.ttec.com/articles/real-time-marketing-analytics-customer-data-optimization-best-practices

FHG. (2022, March 8). *21 chatbot statistics.* LinkedIn. https://www.linkedin.com/pulse/21-chatbot-statistics-fhg-consultants/

Fima, Z., & Likos, P. (2023, June 16). *How Starbucks could boost profits by putting AI chatbots at its drive-thru windows.* CNBC. https://www.cnbc.

com/2023/06/16/starbucks-could-boost-profits-by-putting-ai-chatbots-at-its-drive-thru-windows.html

Frazier, J. (2023, September 6). Council post: Adapting AI or adieu: The new evolutionary rule and five ways to embrace AI. *Forbes*. https://www.forbes.com/sites/theyec/2023/09/06/adapting-ai-or-adieu-the-new-evolutionary-rule-and-five-ways-to-embrace-ai/?sh=33d80c674c93

Fu, J. (2023, May 3). *Top 12 AI recruiting software and recruiting tools for hiring top talent*. Arc Employer Blog. https://arc.dev/employer-blog/top-10-ai-recruiting-software-and-recruiting-tools/

Future Data Stats. (2024, January 12). *Market size, share, trends & competitive analysis global report 2023-2030*. LinkedIn. https://www.linkedin.com/pulse/ai-personalized-marketing-market-size-share-trends-competitive-wzxif/

Gates, B. (n.d.). *Bill Gates quote*. BrainyQuote. https://www.brainyquote.com/quotes/bill_gates_446483

GDPR. (2018, November 7). *What is GDPR, the EU's new data protection law?* https://gdpr.eu/what-is-gdpr/

Gillis, A. S. (2022). *Security audit*. TechTarget CIO. https://www.techtarget.com/searchcio/definition/security-audit

Goh, F. (2020). *10 companies that failed to innovate, resulting in business failure*. Collective Campus. https://www.collectivecampus.io/blog/10-companies-that-were-too-slow-to-respond-to-change

Green, J. (2023, February 23). *Major companies are using AI to avoid bias and cliches in advertising*. Bloomberg. https://www.bloomberg.com/news/newsletters/2023-02-23/major-companies-are-using-ai-to-avoid-bias-and-cliches-in-advertising

Gruber, J. (2020, December 18). *Steve Jobs on privacy*. Daring Fireball. https://daringfireball.net/linked/2020/12/18/steve-jobs-on-privacy

The Guardian. (2018, October 10). Amazon ditched AI recruiting tool that favored men for technical jobs. https://www.theguardian.com/technology/2018/oct/10/amazon-hiring-ai-gender-bias-recruiting-engine

Guinness, H. (2019, December 17). *The 4 best chatbot builders*. Zapier. https://zapier.com/blog/best-chatbot-builders/

Gulhane, A. (2023, June 30). *The future of remote work*. LinkedIn. https://www.linkedin.com/pulse/future-remote-work-akshay-gulhane/

Gupta, A. (2023, March 29). *The AI revolution in a modern enterprise: Driving competitive advantage and growth*. HCLSoftware. https://www.hclsoftware.com/blog/hclsoftware/the-ai-revolution-in-a-modern-enterprise-driving-competitive-advantage-and-growth/

Haan, K. (2023, December 11). *24 top AI statistics and trends in 2024. Forbes.* https://www.forbes.com/advisor/business/ai-statistics/

Hameed, H. (2023, September 11). *Hyper-personalization: Personalization taken to the next level.* commercetools. https://commercetools.com/blog/for-an-online-shopping-experience-more-tailored-than-your-favorite-outfit-try-hyper-personalization

Harmon, A. (2023). *Pros and cons of using AI in recruiting.* Recruiter.com. https://www.recruiter.com/recruiting/pros-and-cons-of-using-ai-in-recruiting/

Hempel, J. (2018, November 13). *Fei-Fei Li's quest to make AI better for humanity.* WIRED. https://www.wired.com/story/fei-fei-li-artificial-intelligence-humanity/

Hobson, N. (2021). *Steve Jobs said what separates a leader from a follower really comes down to this mindset.* INC.Africa. https://www.incafrica.com/article/nick-hobson-steve-jobs-said-what-separates-a-leader-from-a-follower-really-comes-down-to-this-mindset/?source_category=icons++innovators

Holston, A. (2023, May 26). *Addressing bias in AI: Challenges and strategies for IT professionals.* LinkedIn. https://www.linkedin.com/pulse/addressing-bias-ai-challenges-strategies-alexander-holston-md/

Horiachko, A. (2023, June 16). *How to build your own AI chatbot with ChatGPT API: A step-by-step ultimate guide.* Softermii. https://www.softermii.com/blog/how-to-build-your-own-ai-chatbot-with-chatgpt-api-a-step-by-step-ultimate-guide

The Horton Group. (2023, July 11). *Benefits and risks of leveraging AI in employment decisions.* https://www.thehortongroup.com/resources/benefits-and-risks-of-leveraging-ai-in-employment-decisions/

HubSpot. (2020, March 9). *Create a bot.* https://knowledge.hubspot.com/chatflows/create-a-bot

HubSpot. (2024). *Automate conversations with a free chatbot builder.* https://www.hubspot.com/products/crm/chatbot-builder

Hunkenschroer, A. L., & Kriebitz, A. (2022). Is AI recruiting (un)ethical? A human rights perspective on the use of AI for hiring. *AI and Ethics, 3*(1), 199–213. https://doi.org/10.1007/s43681-022-00166-4

Huschka, R. (2023, April 21). *Your industrial AI checklist: 10 things you need to get started.* Automate. https://www.automate.org/ai/industry-insights/your-industrial-ai-checklist-10-things-you-need-to-get-started

Hyperight. (2021, June 30). *Deep brew: Transforming Starbucks into an AI & data-driven company.* https://hyperight.com/deep-brew-transforming-starbucks-into-a-data-driven-company/

Intense Technologies Limited. (2023, October 5). *Staying ahead of the curve: Fostering an innovative culture with AI in IT services better agility & growth in companies.* LinkedIn. https://www.linkedin.com/pulse/staying-ahead-curve-fostering-innovative-culture/

Jackson, J. (2020). *Top 15 key customer engagement metrics to measure.* Dialpad. https://www.dialpad.com/blog/customer-engagement-metrics/

Jain, M. (2020). *Making chatbots more transparent and applicable to new demographics* [Doctoral dissertation, University of Washington]. University Libraries. https://digital.lib.washington.edu/researchworks/bitstream/handle/1773/45928/Jain_washington_0250E_21811.pdf

Jones, K. (2024). *Top AI recruiting tools and software of 2024.* TechTarget HR Software. https://www.techtarget.com/searchhrsoftware/tip/Top-AI-recruiting-tools-and-software-of-2022

Jones, S. (2021, December 6). *Drawbacks of traditional hiring methods and why they no longer work.* Uplers. https://www.uplers.com/blog/drawbacks-of-traditional-hiring-methods/

Kalinin, K. (2023, October 10). *How to make a chatbot from scratch and grow your business with AI.* Topflight Apps. https://topflightapps.com/ideas/how-to-build-a-chatbot/#3

Kaput, M. (2024, January 26). *How Spotify uses AI (And what you can learn from it).* Marketing AI Institute. https://www.marketingaiinstitute.com/blog/spotify-artificial-intelligence

Kent, G. (n.d.). *A quote by Germany Kent.* Goodreads. https://www.goodreads.com/quotes/10918421-cancel-culture-is-a-real-thing-your-digital-footprint-is

Kenton, W. (2023, October 30). *SWOT analysis: How to with table and example.* Investopedia. https://www.investopedia.com/terms/s/swot.asp

Kerry, C. F. (2020, February 10). *Protecting privacy in an AI-driven world.* Brookings. https://www.brookings.edu/articles/protecting-privacy-in-an-ai-driven-world/

Kidd, C. (2022, November 29). *Data encryption methods & types: Beginner's guide to encryption.* Splunk. https://www.splunk.com/en_us/blog/learn/data-encryption-methods-types.html

Kingdom Security. (2024). *The best physical security measures to safeguard your business.* https://www.kingdom.co.uk/blog/physical-security-measures-to-safeguard-your-business

Kovacs, G. (n.d.). *Gary Kovacs quote.* BrainyQuote. https://www.brainyquote.com/quotes/gary_kovacs_555281

Krishnan, V. (2020, July 20). *How to create a small business budget in 8 simple steps.* Zoho Books. https://www.zoho.com/books/guides/how-to-create-a-realistic-business-budget.html

Kumar, D. (2022, July 21). *Implementing customer segmentation using machine learning [beginners guide].* Neptune.ai. https://neptune.ai/blog/customer-segmentation-using-machine-learning

Kuppannan, R. (2023, June 16). *Essential checklist before adopting AI/ML in your organization.* LinkedIn. https://www.linkedin.com/pulse/essential-checklist-before-adopting-aiml-your-ragu/

Kutarenko, S., & Ampilogova, A. (2023, January 11). *Conversational AI: Real-world examples, use cases, and benefits.* Trinetix. https://www.trinetix.com/insights/conversational-ai-examples-and-use-cases

Landry, L. (2019, February 14). *4 startup challenges to avoid when scaling your business.* Business Insights Blog. https://online.hbs.edu/blog/post/scaling-startup-challenges-to-avoid

Lange, C. (2023, June 2). *Hyper-personalization: Unleashing the next level of customer engagement in marketing.* LinkedIn. https://www.linkedin.com/pulse/hyper-personalization-unleashing-next-level-customer-engagement/

Langeland, J. (2023, August 14). *GDPR in the US: Compliance simplified for businesses.* Termly. https://termly.io/resources/articles/gdpr-in-the-us/

Leah. (2022, December 6). *Chatbot case studies: Real-life results across industries.* Userlike. https://www.userlike.com/en/blog/chatbot-case-studies

LeBruce, I. (2024, January 7). *Revolutionizing recruitment: An AI case study.* X0PA AI. https://x0pa.com/blog/revolutionizing-recruitment-an-ai-case-study/

Leonard, K., & Watts, R. (2022, May 11). The ultimate guide to S.M.A.R.T. goals. *Forbes.* https://www.forbes.com/advisor/business/smart-goals/

Likhadzed, V., & Klubnikin, A. (2024, February 19). *How much does AI cost in 2024? Well, it depends.* ITRex. https://itrexgroup.com/blog/how-much-does-artificial-intelligence-cost/

LiveAgent. (2023, July 31). *Marketing audit checklist - A guide to effective analysis.* https://www.liveagent.com/checklists/marketing-audit-checklist/

LivePerson. (2023, February 27). *Conversational AI readiness: Checklist for success.* https://www.liveperson.com/blog/ai-readiness-checklist/

Lomas, N. (2020, June 10). *Babylon Health admits "software error" led to patient data breach.* TechCrunch. https://techcrunch.com/2020/06/10/babylon-health-admits-software-error-led-to-patient-data-breach/?guccounter=2

Lucas, E. (2023, October 5). Five AI tools to help with your job search—or with helping you quit. *Forbes.* https://www.forbes.com/sites/emmylucas/2023/07/17/five-ai-tools-to-help-with-your-job-search-or-with-helping-you-quit/?sh=12225722372c

Mainstay. (2019, September 16). *40% of students don't get assistance for their mental health issues. Can chatbots help?* https://mainstay.com/blog/how-chatbots-handle-sensitive-topics/

Makarenko, E. (2021, February 24). *What is conversational AI and what is its impact on businesses?* Master of Code Global. https://masterofcode.com/blog/the-impact-of-conversational-ai-2021-and-forward

Mandal, A. (2021, June 22). *The algorithmic origins of bias.* Feminist AI. https://feministai.pubpub.org/pub/the-algorithmic-origins-of-bias/release/3

Marinaki, A. (2020, February 27). *Digital transformation of recruitment: How can you benefit?* Resources for Employers. https://resources.workable.com/stories-and-insights/digital-transformation-of-recruitment

Mark. (2023, March 10). *ChatGPT API pricing - Ten times cheaper than GPT-3.5.* MLYearning. https://www.mlyearning.org/chatgpt-api-pricing/

MarketingSherpa. (2022, October 31). *Artificial intelligence case studies: Two companies that boosted brand awareness with AI and another marketer that used humans instead.* https://www.marketingsherpa.com/article/case-study/artificial-intelligence

Marr, B. (2021, July 2). *How to develop an artificial intelligence strategy: 9 things every business must include.* Bernard Marr. https://bernardmarr.com/how-to-develop-an-artificial-intelligence-strategy-9-things-every-business-must-include/

Marr, B. (2024, February 20). The 10 most important AI trends for 2024 everyone must be ready for now. *Forbes.* https://www.forbes.com/sites/bernardmarr/2023/09/18/the-10-most-important-ai-trends-for-2024-everyone-must-be-ready-for-now/?sh=5f87fe0d36bd

Marston, R. (n.d.). *Ralph Marston quote.* BrainyQuote. https://www.

brainyquote.com/quotes/ralph_marston_125719

Master of Code Global. (2021, March 12). *Conversational AI in ecommerce: 9 of the most successful chatbot examples*. Medium. https://masterofcodeglobal.medium.com/conversational-ai-in-ecommerce-9-of-the-most-successful-chatbot-examples-89bc5e1569b3

Maya HTT. (n.d.). *AI-readiness assessment*. SurveyMonkey. https://www.surveymonkey.com/r/395XY2N

McCann, A. (2023, August 10). *How to use AI for recruitment*. Resources for Employers. https://resources.workable.com/tutorial/ai-for-recruitment

Medairy, B. (2021). *4 ways to preserve privacy in artificial intelligence*. Booz Allen Hamilton. https://www.boozallen.com/s/solution/four-ways-to-preserve-privacy-in-ai.html

Mehta, R. (2023, June 12). *The anatomy of a pivot*. Ravi Mehta. https://www.ravi-mehta.com/the-anatomy-of-a-pivot/

Mercier, M. (2022, September 6). *ROI for chatbots*. Botpress. https://botpress.com/blog/roi-for-chatbots

Michael, C. (2023, March 2). *A layperson's guide to understanding Chat GPT's token-based pricing*. Medium. https://mcengkuru.medium.com/a-laypersons-guide-to-understanding-chat-gpt-s-token-based-pricing-fee340d504c8

Microsoft. (2022, February 7). *AI fairness checklist*. https://www.microsoft.com/en-us/research/project/ai-fairness-checklist/

MindTools Content Team. (2024). *SWOT analysis*. MindTools. https://www.mindtools.com/amtbj63/swot-analysis

MIT Technology Review Insights. (2021, May 19). *Embracing the rapid pace of AI*. MIT Technology Review. https://www.technologyreview.com/2021/05/19/1025016/embracing-the-rapid-pace-of-ai/

MoEngage. (2023, December 13). *13 metrics you have to measure in 2024*. https://www.moengage.com/learn/customer-engagement-metrics-with-examples/

Mohammed, S. (2023, February 23). *AI-powered customer segmentation: How to unlock hidden opportunities*. Medium. https://shahmm.medium.com/ai-powered-customer-segmentation-how-to-unlock-hidden-opportunities-eb4124705d72

Moss, W. (2023, March 14). *Hiring black tech talent - A case study in success leveraging diversity recruitment events with HBCU CONNECT*. LinkedIn. https://www.linkedin.com/pulse/hiring-black-tech-talent-case-study-success-leveraging-will-moss/

MTS Staff Writer. (2023, February 28). *Bias in AI: What biases do* marketers/advertisers need to be careful about. MarTech Series. https://martechseries.com/mts-insights/staff-writers/bias-in-ai-what-biases-do-marketers-advertisers-need-to-be-careful-about/

Murphy, J. (2023). *How businesses can measure AI success with KPIs.* TechTarget Enterprise AI. https://www.techtarget.com/searchenterpriseai/tip/How-businesses-can-measure-AI-success-with-KPIs

Naik, N. (2023, October 5). Council post: How artificial intelligence benefits recruiting. *Forbes.* https://www.forbes.com/sites/forbesbusinesscouncil/2023/06/01/how-artificial-intelligence-benefits-recruiting/?sh=6dbb94587f22

Naik, N. (2023, October 5). Council post: How artificial intelligence benefits recruiting. *Forbes.* https://www.forbes.com/sites/forbesbusinesscouncil/2023/06/01/how-artificial-intelligence-benefits-recruiting/?sh=ac379977f226

Nelson, R. (2017, November 7). *10 case studies on chatbots.* Overthink Group. https://overthinkgroup.com/chatbot-case-studies/

Nilormi, D. (2023, May 15). *How to stay relevant in an age of AI?* LinkedIn. https://www.linkedin.com/pulse/how-stay-relevant-age-ai-nilormi-das/

Norris, P. (2023, April 13). *18 impressive examples of AI in marketing.* Social Media Strategies Summit Blog. https://blog.socialmediastrategiessummit.com/10-examples-of-ai-in-marketing/

O'Connor, N. (2023, July 26). *The AI bot buyer's guide: How to find the right AI chatbot for your support needs.* The Intercom Blog. https://www.intercom.com/blog/ai-bot-buyers-guide/

Oplinger, A. (2023, September 22). *Aligning AI driven objectives with business goals: A strategic approach.* RafterOne. https://www.rafter.one/aligning-ai-driven-objectives-with-business-goals-a-strategic-approach/

Orza, P. (2022). *How to use AI for marketing.* Levity.ai. https://levity.ai/blog/how-to-use-ai-for-marketing-benefits-examples

Osipov, A. (2023, June 25). *Starbucks and the power of AI marketing.* LinkedIn. https://www.linkedin.com/pulse/starbucks-power-ai-marketing-anton-osipov/

Outbox Recruitment. (2023, June 5). *Building trust in the recruitment industry and pricing transparency.* LinkedIn. https://www.linkedin.com/pulse/building-trust-recruitment-industry-pricing-transparency/

Pathak, R. (2023, May 1). *The importance of regular security audits in today's* digital landscape. LinkedIn. https://www.linkedin.com/pulse/importance-regular-security-audits-todays-digital-landscape-pathak/

Perry, E. (2023, June 15). *Vision boards: What are they & how to create one in 5 steps*. BetterUp. https://www.betterup.com/blog/how-to-create-vision-board

Phillips, A. (2024, March 11). *11 AI marketing tools your team should be using in 2024*. Sprout Social. https://sproutsocial.com/insights/ai-marketing-tools/

Pointon, A. (2023, June 14). *Benefits of cultivating a culture change*. Aspirant. https://www.aspirant.com/blog/culture-change-benefits

Potor, M. (2023, June 29). *AI chatbot examples: These 9 companies get it right!* Sinch Engage. https://engage.sinch.com/blog/ai-chatbot-examples-these-9-companies-get-it-right/

Pratchett, T. (n.d.). *Terry Pratchett quote*. Goodreads. https://www.goodreads.com/quotes/35011-it-s-still-magic-even-if-you-know-how-it-s-done

Pratt, M. K. (2023). *12 key benefits of AI for business*. TechTarget Enterprise AI. https://www.techtarget.com/searchenterpriseai/feature/6-key-benefits-of-AI-for-business

PwC. (2017). *Case study: Chatbot*. https://www.pwc.co.uk/industries/financial-services/fs-case-study-chatbot.html

Qualitrol Corp. (2023, July 12). *Pilot testing of AI algorithm for fault record analysis*. https://www.qualitrolcorp.com/pilot-testing-of-ai-algorithm-for-fault-record-analysis/

Ram, R. (2023, July 12). *How to stay updated on AI development and AI News: Essential tools and techniques*. LinkedIn. https://www.linkedin.com/pulse/how-stay-updated-ai-development-news-essential-tools-techniques-ram/

Recruiters LineUp. (2024, January 3). *10 best AI recruiting tools of 2024*. https://www.recruiterslineup.com/10-best-ai-recruiting-tools-of-2022/

Retta, L. (2024, April 2). *15 great quotes that will inspire you to start optimizing*. Dynamic Yield. https://www.dynamicyield.com/article/15-quotes/

Revartis. (2024). *The ROI of AI: How artificial intelligence delivers tangible business value*. https://revartis.com/insight/the-roi-of-ai-how-artificial-intelligence-delivers-tangible-business-value/

Rock Content Writer. (2023, April 19). *Everything you need to know about ChatGPT bias*. Rock Content. https://rockcontent.com/blog/chatgpt-bias/

Rodriguez, I. (2021, August 18). *Tech stack: Definition + 9 examples from the world's top brands*. HubSpot. https://blog.hubspot.com/customers/auditing-your-companys-tech-stack-or-platform-apps

Rometty, G. (n.d.). *A quote by Ginni Romerty*. BrainyQuote. https://www.brainyquote.com/quotes/ginni_rometty_806891

Ross, L., & Epifano, M. (2024, January 8). *9 companies that failed to adapt to disruption and paid the ultimate price*. Thomasnet.com. https://www.thomasnet.com/insights/7-companies-that-failed-to-adapt-to-disruption-and-paid-the-ultimate-price/

Saab, H. (2023, April 22). *The accelerating pace of AI progress and the demands for rapid adaptation*. LinkedIn. https://www.linkedin.com/pulse/accelerating-pace-ai-progress-demands-rapid-adaptation-hussein-saab/

Sams, A. (2022, March 10). *4 incredible AI case studies in content marketing*. Marketing AI Institute. https://www.marketingaiinstitute.com/blog/ai-case-studies-content-marketing

Samuel, P. (2023, December 18). *Artificial intelligence (AI) statistics for small business in 2024*. ColorWhistle. https://colorwhistle.com/artificial-intelligence-statistics-for-small-business/

Sangwan, D. (2023, July 10). *Case study: Harnessing AI for personalized customer experiences: StarBucks' success story*. LinkedIn. https://www.linkedin.com/pulse/case-study-harnessing-ai-personalized-customer-success-deepak-sangwan/

Sangwoo, S. (2023, April 17). *The success of AI depends on the speed of iteration: An MLOps strategy for AI models in manufacturing*. MLOps Community. https://mlops.community/the-success-of-ai-depends-on-the-speed-of-iteration-an-mlops-strategy-for-ai-models-in-manufacturing/

Sankarapu, V. K. (2023, October 5). Council post: The result of unchecked AI: Balancing the benefits and the risks. *Forbes*. https://www.forbes.com/sites/forbestechcouncil/2023/05/26/the-result-of-unchecked-ai-balancing-the-benefits-and-the-risks/?sh=1c2e5883ff19

Satori Cyber. (2022, November 22). *Data anonymization: Use cases and 6 common techniques*. https://satoricyber.com/data-masking/data-anonymization-use-cases-and-6-common-techniques/

Serpa, Y. (2020, July 23). *How I stay updated on the latest AI research*. Towards Data Science. https://towardsdatascience.com/how-i-stay-updated-on-the-latest-ai-research-b81203155551

Shalini, L. (2020, March 30). *Traditional methods of recruitment versus modern methods of recruitment*. GoBetter Blog. https://go-better.com/blog/traditional-vs-modern-recruitment/

Sharma, V. (2023, April 6). *"Traditional vs non-traditional recruitment methods: Finding the right fit for your company."* LinkedIn. https://www.linkedin.com/pulse/traditional-vs-non-traditional-recruitment-methods-finding-sharma/

Sheth, B. (2023, October 5). Council post: Ways to boost customer engagement using conversational AI. *Forbes*. https://www.forbes.com/sites/forbestechcouncil/2021/08/04/ways-to-boost-customer-engagement-using-conversational-ai/?sh=348fa4db59ab

Siegel, J. (2024). *The ethical implications of the chatbot user experience*. Bentley University. https://www.bentley.edu/centers/user-experience-center/ethical-implications-chatbot-user-experience

SmartAsset. (2024). *Free budget calculator*. https://smartasset.com/mortgage/budget-calculator

Southern, M. G. (2023, December 4). *Google Bard director talks usage, ethics, and competitive advantage*. Search Engine Journal. https://www.searchenginejournal.com/google-bard-director-talks-usage-ethics-and-competitive-advantage/502965/

Spair, R. (2023, October 9). *The art of measuring the ROI of AI*. LinkedIn. https://www.linkedin.com/pulse/art-measuring-roi-ai-rick-spair-/

Sparks, S. (2023, August 10). *How to evaluate AI and recruitment automation software*. Jobvite. https://www.jobvite.com/blog/recruitment-automation-software/

Spataro, J. (2023, June 28). *3 steps to prepare your culture for AI*. Harvard Business Review. https://hbr.org/2023/06/3-steps-to-prepare-your-culture-for-ai

Sprinklr. (2023, July 25). *15 best chatbot examples from groundbreaking brands*. https://www.sprinklr.com/blog/chatbot-examples/

Sprout Social. (2024, February 28). *The role of artificial intelligence in marketing*. https://sproutsocial.com/insights/ai-marketing/

Srikanth, A. (2022, April 4). *Product customization: Benefits, examples, & tips*. Freshdesk Blog. https://www.freshworks.com/freshdesk/general/product-customization-for-customer-satisfaction-blog/

Srivastava, S. (2023, October 5). *7 top-rated AI-enabled tools for recruiters*. Capterra. https://www.capterra.com/resources/ai-recruiting-tools/

Staffing Referrals. (2020, October 19). *How recruitment automation frees up your recruiters' time*. https://staffingreferrals.com/blog/7-automations-that-free-up-your-recruiters-time/

Stanke, B. (2023, February 15). *How AI can help develop a strategic plan*. BOB STANKE. https://www.bobstanke.com/blog/ai-for-strategic-planning

Sunscrapers Team. (2023, May 22). *5 best practices for ethical data sourcing in the age of big data*. Sunscrapers. https://sunscrapers.com/blog/5-best-practices-for-ethical-data-sourcing-in-the-age-of-big-data/

Talent2Win. (2021, October 19). *Difference between modern and traditional recruitment methods*. https://talent2win.com/talent-acquisition-recruitment-methods/

Tarasov, A., & Shynkarenko, P. (2023, September 8). *5 steps for assembling AI-driven business teams*. TechCrunch. https://techcrunch.com/2023/09/08/5-steps-for-assembling-ai-driven-business-teams/

Taskade. (2024). *Personal vision board template*. https://www.taskade.com/templates/personal/personal-vision-board

Taylor, C. (2023a, October 5). How artificial intelligence is helping today's small businesses. *Forbes*. https://www.forbes.com/sites/charlesrtaylor/2023/08/09/how-artificial-intelligence-is-helping-todays-small-businesses/?sh=4c5d23281a48

Taylor, C. (2023b, October 6). *How to use AI to refresh old blog content*. Search Engine Land. https://searchengineland.com/use-ai-refresh-old-blog-content-432945

Tenable. (2022). *Understanding cyber threats in today's digital world*. https://www.tenable.com/principles/cyber-threats-principles

Tiffany. (2023, December 26). *50 chatbot statistics crucial to know in 2024*. ChatInsight. https://www.chatinsight.ai/chatbots/chatbot-statistics/

Top Echelon. (2023, March 10). *Running a search*. https://topechelon.com/placement-process/10-ways-protect-candidate-data-recruiting-process/

Turits, M., & Crawford, H. (2021, April 23). *How to create a business budget for your small business*. NerdWallet. https://www.nerdwallet.com/article/small-business/how-to-create-a-business-budget

Uzialko, A. (2019, April 22). *How artificial intelligence will transform businesses*. Business News Daily. https://www.businessnewsdaily.com/9402-artificial-intelligence-business-trends.html

Valuer. (2022, July 28). *50 brands that failed to innovate*. https://www.valuer.ai/blog/50-examples-of-corporations-that-failed-to-innovate-and-missed-their-chance

van Bekkum, M., & Borgesius, F. Z. (2023). Using sensitive data to prevent discrimination by artificial intelligence: Does the GDPR need a new exception? *Computer Law & Security Review, 48,* 105770–105770. https://doi.org/10.1016/j.clsr.2022.105770

Vicente, V. (2023, April 19). *Security audits: A comprehensive overview.* AuditBoard. https://www.auditboard.com/blog/what-is-security-audit/

Villanova University. (2019, September 3). *How to establish transparency to improve talent acquisition.* https://www.villanovau.com/articles/hr/transparency-talent-acquisition/

Vincent, J. (2023, April 19). *Google employees label AI chatbot Bard "worse than useless" and "a pathological liar": Report.* The Verge. https://www.theverge.com/2023/4/19/23689554/google-ai-chatbot-bard-employees-criticism-pathological-liar

Voxturr. (2020, February 3). *Top 7 chatbot case studies that growth hacked businesses {updated 2021}.* https://voxturr.com/chatbot-case-studies-that-growth-hacked-businesses/

Wang, E. (2023, July 28). *7 tips to prepare your team for the AI future.* Xembly.com. https://www.xembly.com/resources/7-tips-to-prepare-your-team-for-the-ai-future

Westwater, S. (2023, November 20). *AI marketing case study: Discover success stories and cutting-edge strategies.* Pragmatic. https://www.pragmatic.digital/blog/ai-marketing-case-study-successful-campaigns

Wiles, J., & Perri, L. (2022, October 27). *Why adaptive AI should matter to your business.* Gartner. https://www.gartner.com/en/articles/why-adaptive-ai-should-matter-to-your-business

Wilkinson, L. (2023, March). *OpenAI lowers ChatGPT API price.* CIO Dive. https://www.ciodive.com/news/OpenAI-ChatGPT-Whisper-API-data-privacy/643921/

WIZ.AI. (2024, January 4). *What is the artificial intelligence revolution and why does it matter to your business?* https://www.wiz.ai/what-is-the-artificial-intelligence-revolution-and-why-does-it-matter-to-your-business/

Włodarczyk, K. (2023, August 30). *Embracing agile for successful AI and ML projects.* Sunscrapers. https://sunscrapers.com/blog/agile-for-ai-ml-project-success/

Wren, H. (2020, September 18). *7 ways to reduce bias in conversational AI.* Zendesk. https://www.zendesk.com/blog/7-ways-reduce-bias-conversational-ai/

YouCanDealWithIt. (n.d.). *Budget calculator.* http://www.youcandealwithit.com/calculators/budget-calculator

Young, C. (2023, July 14). *Build a winning AI strategy for your business.* Harvard Business Review. https://hbr.org/2023/07/build-a-winning-ai-strategy-for-your-business

Zaremba, Y. (2024, February 2). *Data privacy and compliance for marketers: A complete guide.* Improvado. https://improvado.io/blog/data-privacy-and-compliance-for-marketers-guide

www.ingramcontent.com/pod-product-compliance
Lightning Source LLC
Chambersburg PA
CBHW071915210526
45479CB00002B/431